THE BROKEN COUNTRY

THE BROKEN COUNTRY

On Trauma,
a Crime, and the
Continuing Legacy
of Vietnam

Paisley Rekdal

THE UNIVERSITY OF GEORGIA PRESS

ATHENS

© 2017 by the University of Georgia Press

Athens, Georgia 30602

www.ugapress.org

All rights reserved

Designed by Erin Kirk New

Set in 10 on 15 Chapparal

Printed and bound by Thomson-Shore, Inc.

The paper in this book meets the guidelines for
permanence and durability of the Committee on
Production Guidelines for Book Longevity of the
Council on Library Resources.

Most University of Georgia Press titles are
available from popular e-book vendors.

Printed in the United States of America

21 20 19 18 17 C 5 4 3 2 1

Library of Congress Control Number: 2017947226

ISBN: 9780820351179 (paperback)

ISBN: 9780820351186 (ebook)

For my father, my uncles, and all those touched by war

ACKNOWLEDGMENTS

Any book is supported by a cast of dozens: in this case, it was closer to a cast of hundreds. First, thanks to Michael Steinberg and Thomas Larson for reading and selecting the book for the AWP Prize for Creative Nonfiction, and to all the editors, designers, copyeditors, and publicists at the University of Georgia Press for ushering it into the world, specifically Thomas Roche and Dorine Jennette for their tremendous help in fine-tuning the manuscript. Thanks to Mark Schwartz for pulling all the many trial dates for Kiet Thanh Ly, and for his legal help in interpreting some of the particulars of Ly's case. Thanks to Jensen Private Investigations. Thanks to Mimi Khúc, Lawrence-Minh Bùi Davis, and the *Asian American Literary Review* for publishing a section of the book in their issue devoted to Asian American mental health issues. Thanks to Ellen Umansky for publishing another short section as a feature essay on the Poetry Foundation website. Thanks also to *Blackbird* and its editors for publishing the first chapter. Enormous thanks to Vincent Cheng, Melanie Rae Thon, and Emma Parry for giving early, or late, reads of the manuscript and for offering sound criticism, smart edits, and excellent advice.

Thanks to the many people I spoke to about this project who generously offered me their contacts, insights, stories, and time: Keltin Barney, Tim DeJulis, Mike DeJulis, Doug Duncan, Susanne Gipson, Mai-Linh Hong, Keven Lee, Trinh Mai, Jeff Nay, Cuong Nguyen, Diana Khoi Nguyen, Linh Nguyen, Duoc Pham, Diana Phuong, Amie Rosenberg, and Plum Schultz. Thanks to my colleagues in the Asia Center, in particular Winston Kyan and Wesley Sasaki-Uemura for their suggestions, personal and theoretical perspectives, and encouragement. Thanks, too, to Gregory Smoak, Vicky Newman, and the American West Center, for sharing with me the oral histories of Vietnam War veterans and Southeast Asian refugees found in its *Saving the Legacy: An Oral History of Utah's Veterans Archive*. Thanks to Jennifer Chang for her insights and contacts. And thanks also to colleagues and friends Jenny Andrus and Casey Boyle, who sent me in the direction of investigating violence and rhetoric.

Enormous thanks for the financial and creative support offered me by the Amy Lowell Poetry Travelling Scholarship, the John Simon Guggenheim Memorial Foundation, the University of Utah, and the University of Utah University Research Committee. Without the support and time granted me by these institutions, it is doubtful I could have even considered writing this book, let alone transcribed the hours of interviews.

Thanks to my ever-supporting and ever-patient husband, Sean Myles, who, without complaint, got take-out, walked the dog, and gave me the hours alone to write this book.

Finally, thanks to my father, Thomas Rekdal, my uncle Kingsley Kan, my cousin Jonathan Kan, and all of the many other men in my family who have served our country. This book is for them.

THE BROKEN COUNTRY

1

It is early afternoon in late April, and Keltin Barney is walking across a parking lot toward the glassed entrance of Smith's Marketplace. Keltin, a thirty-year-old undergraduate at the University of Utah, is running an errand for his girlfriend, Elizabeth, who has tasked him with buying two pairs of bicycle tire inserts and a storage unit lock. Located between the university where Keltin studies English and downtown Salt Lake City, the Smith's that Keltin has chosen is the city's most popular megastore, selling everything from electronics to sushi, cheap produce to children's shoes. The store is full today, and customers flow steadily through the parking lot: mothers with angry toddlers, groups of teens, young men and women off work from a nearby construction site, the occasional temporarily flush panhandler. On the store's grassy parking strip, several feet from the entrance, a homeless man sits cross-legged, a Smith's grocery cart beside him stacked with garbage sacks of clothing, a cardboard sign in his hand that reads, "Veteran. Please help."

The late afternoon sun is fierce. The cool noon temperature has slowly heated up under a thick blanket of clouds that traps the sun but blocks any breeze, turning the air into a muggy broth. Salt Lake is forty-three hundred feet above sea level: the city's thin air and intense sun mean that even on a mildly warm day, a person can begin to feel slow roasted. Keltin is fair skinned and strawberry blond. He has lashes so pale they look white against his blue eyes, and his skin has already begun to pink. He squints into the glare off the rows of car windshields, the glass that lines the entrance to the store. To his right, a line of cars glides through the Wendy's drive-through. He has just reached the entrance to the store when he realizes he's forgotten the list Elizabeth drew up for him. Unsure what size tubes to purchase, he takes out his phone, dials his girlfriend, and walks back to his car.

It isn't until he's reaching for the list on the passenger seat that he hears a man's voice behind him say, "Hey." Keltin straightens, turns, and sees an Asian man around his age wearing a nubbed wool sweater and three thin coats. The man's face is impassive, his dark eyes blank as a shark's, but his hair is stiff with grease and dust, the browned skin of his hands seamed with dirt. Keltin has just registered the oddness—three jackets and a sweater at the end of April?—when he feels the stranger shove him, pushing hard at the base of his sternum.

Only the stranger hasn't pushed Keltin. Blood has begun to pump from Keltin's chest, darkening his shirt and running down his arms, soaking his pants. Keltin can't feel any pain, but the blood is warm and pulsing, and as the stranger jumps toward him, he begins to run. He leaps backward, scuttling behind his open car door to put something between him and this stranger, but the man has begun swinging his fist wildly at Keltin: at his back and sides, at his left arm. Something flashes in the man's fist. Keltin shouts in surprise, blood rushing in a thick gush from his left arm, until somehow he's away from his attacker, half-dashing, half-stumbling toward the glass entrance of the store.

The man is chasing him, or not; Keltin isn't sure. He's focused on the entrance to Smith's: he wants to get someone's attention, to disappear into the crowd. But though the parking lot is full of shoppers, no one has stepped forward to help, shocked or terrified as they are by Keltin's incoherent shouts, which is when he realizes he's still holding his cell phone. His girlfriend, Elizabeth, has heard everything, though she doesn't understand what she's hearing.

"I'm stabbed," he yells, five, thirty incoherent times into the phone, until he's finally able to make himself understood. "A man just stabbed me!" he shouts at Elizabeth, who is by now screaming herself, begging him to stay put. She works a few blocks away at the Sam Weller's bookstore in Trolley Square, a quaintly historic, upmarket minimall in the city's old trolley station, where just five years earlier a mentally disturbed Bosnian immigrant had shot and killed five people. It's a hard run between stores, but a quick drive: she's already yelling for a coworker to get his car.

Keltin has dropped the phone. He's staggered into the glassed-in entranceway now at Smith's, swaying in the cool, air-conditioned antechamber beside a line of shopping carts. People are everywhere, some running through the sliding doors past him to get back into the store, one or two others rushing to the parking lot, where Keltin assumes his attacker must be. Keltin stays where he is, looking over his injuries. He's too stunned to do more than look: he sways on his feet, aware of his attacker's movements only through the frenzied activity of other shoppers gathered in the lot. People scatter, the crowd opens, and he sees his attacker lunge at a man who, luckily, is close enough to his car that he's able to use his driver's side door as a shield before ducking into the driver's seat, locking the door, and digging out his cell phone. Keltin's attacker turns and lunges toward another man, someone much taller than him—the homeless man rears suddenly upward, one arm raised, then plunges the blade into his victim's eye.

Keltin slides to the floor. Exhaustion throbs through his body. His left arm is a coursing faucet of flood, the dark red pumping out of the crook of his elbow. He puts a hand out to steady himself and feels cold radiating up from the cracked linoleum beneath his fingertips. Taylor Swift's "Today Was a Fairytale" whines above him. Keltin unloops the belt from his jeans with his right arm and tries to twist it around his left in a makeshift tourniquet. He hears the snick of the interior glass doors sliding open, and Keltin looks up to see the tall, dark, slightly stooped figure of his classmate, Jeff Nay, loping toward him. Keltin blinks but is not surprised: this is Salt Lake City, after all, a town so small that even when a homeless man tries to kill you, someone you know will wander by to witness it. Jeff's black hair swings into his face as he bends to touch Keltin. He pauses as he takes in the belt, looped in a weak knot over Keltin's arm. Keltin holds up an edge of the belt and stammers, "Tourniquet." Jeff nods, points to the blood, and says, "I think you need to lie down."

Keltin has lost a lot of blood. Blood streams from his arm, both sides of his torso, the back of his shoulder, his chest, his cheek. The homeless man who attacked him, Kiet Thanh Ly, stabbed him nine times in the space of two minutes. The push Keltin felt while standing by his car was the force of a serrated blade being punched into the base of his sternum, all the way up to the knife's hilt. Then Ly twisted the knife so that the blade ran parallel to the ground, puncturing bone and tissue but, miraculously, missing all of Keltin's vital organs. Keltin will wear a large L-shaped scar on his chest, and he will also have a small, scythe-shaped scar on his left cheek near his nose, exactly at the base of his cheekbone, so that it will look like he is perpetually on the verge of smiling. Ly stabbed both Keltin's sides in two vicious swipes, which scraped the skin up and off his ribs, places on his body that now feel horribly, frighteningly *wet* to Keltin, as if he were leaking not only blood, but whatever fluids were necessary for his internal organs to survive. It is these wounds that Keltin worries most over, as they are slowly pricking to painful life, the skin of his torso—pushed up by the blade like plaster scraped up by a putty knife—now almost crackling under his T-shirt, though it is his arm that presents the greatest threat. Keltin doesn't know that the knife has punctured clean through his arm, shearing the radial nerve and scraping the ulna; the scar he will later have looks like a thin coil of pale pink beads roped around his left elbow cap. It will take two major surgeries to repair the nerves that have been alternately sliced and frayed during the attack and even then, Keltin's emergency doctor—like Keltin, a former English major, who will joke with Keltin about books in the emergency room just as his mother and girlfriend arrive, tears streaming down their cheeks—will not be sure that Keltin will be able to regain mobility in his hand.

But right now Keltin is lying in a thick wash of his own blood. He can't move his left arm at all now, and the belt is both slick and sticky. *There is no way someone can lose this much blood and survive*, he thinks, and so Keltin knows that he is going to die. He is sure of it. Jeff's grim, determined look confirms this, as does the metallic cold that's now seized one half of his body. He is going to die, and the thought of it is one piercing moment of terror to Keltin, an icy shard that threatens to split him apart, but which, surprisingly, dissolves almost as soon as it penetrates his consciousness. He is going to die, and now a sudden wave of sadness overwhelms him: for Elizabeth, even now rushing toward him in her coworker's car, and for his mother, grieving right now at the bedside of her younger brother, dying himself from liver failure. Neither of them, Keltin knows, will be able to see him a final time, and neither of them are quite resilient enough, he thinks, to process the shock that will accompany his death. He blinks at the ceiling where Jeff's face looms. "You told me I was pretty when I looked like a mess," a girl's tinny voice croons through the shop speakers. Keltin groans and turns his head to focus on the black wheels of the shopping carts.

Outside, Kiet Thanh Ly, Keltin's attacker, is surrounded by people who have blocked off his escape. A man behind Ly swings a backpack at his arms and head, trying to knock him out, but Ly lunges at him with the knife. The young man backs off, but now another stranger rushes in to swing at the back of Ly's head. Ly turns and turns again. The knife he purchased just ten minutes ago from the store, a ten-inch blade he'd had to ask the checkout girl to cut out of its plastic packaging, is slippery. It feels small and useless in his hand, but still the young men around him panic when he shows it to them. One of them drops his pack when Ly slashes, backs away and starts to run. But other people are using bags now, heavy sacks and purses as weapons. Ly turns, slowed by the weight and layers of his clothing, whirls like a clumsy bear, but he can't stop all of them. He can't see all sides at once, all these wide, white mouths and screaming faces. "You killed my people!" he shouts, and the white faces expand; they waver and elongate, their teeth and eyes shivering. "Why did you kill my people?" he moans. From down the block, the screech of sirens echoes toward him.

Suddenly, a large white man materializes with a gun. Ly has seen this man before, jogging purposefully past him to a truck where he reached into the glove compartment. Then, Ly had turned away, busy trying to ward off the blows of another stranger who had snuck up behind him. Now, he sees that this man has a gun, he has both hands on the handle and has raised the weapon to point at Ly's face. The man is telling Ly to drop his knife, to get on the ground. This man must be a soldier. He stands like a soldier. He sounds like a soldier. He is the reason Ly knew he must come and buy a knife. But Ly can't kill him now. He is being told to get on the ground and Ly shakes his head but complies. He slides to the blacktop. The sun is a hot vise on the back of his neck, and when he looks up, everything is white.

Across the parking lot, Keltin is being loaded into an ambulance. His friend, Jeff, has gone now, melted into the crowd. Another ambulance has picked up the man Keltin thought was stabbed through the eye but was actually stabbed in the left side of his head above his ear. His brain has begun to swell, which will require him to undergo an emergency five-hour craniotomy. The damage will obliterate his short-term memory, as well as much of his right-side motor function and language skills. The man, Timothy DeJulis, is in his early forties. A husband and father of two children, he'd recently received his engineering license and changed jobs. He was at the store to buy his son a birthday present, but now will spend the next several months in the hospital and in physical therapy. The brain trauma he sustained will erase his memory of this day, but the attack will return once as a blistering nightmare in which Ly's black-eyed face swims into focus. He will remember that face clearly from this dream, which will prove inadmissible as evidence in court, so that at the pretrial hearing, he'll have to sit on the stand, baffled and discomfited, unable to recognize the other victims from the stabbing, to rely on anything more than a scrap of nightmare for a memory.

But for now, everything is a fuzzy, panic-streaked blur for both men, especially for Keltin, who finds that images from his past and present slip by in flashes, bright and articulated as panels in a comic book. He is aware some other narrative is taking place, something that might fuse these thoughts together, but it lingers just outside the edges of his consciousness. Keltin sees Ly's face: dead-eyed, impassive. Then a flash of Elizabeth appears, then a smeary bank of glass, then his mother.

Keltin lies back. Paramedics are cutting off his shirt now, replacing the makeshift tourniquet with one of their own. Lightning streaks of pain burn through him as his arm is twisted gently back and forth. The paramedics have propped his arm so that his forearm is raised. It is to keep the blood flow down, they tell him. Keltin feels wet and heavy, like ripped meat. Nothing like this has ever happened to him, he thinks, stunned. "Hold your arm like this," one of the paramedics reminds him, moving his drooping arm carefully back in place. "Can you tell me your name? Can you tell me what happened?"

Keltin opens his mouth to answer, but then the pain hits him. Keltin, knocked fully into it, begins screaming.

2 At first, the outlines of the crime seemed to me quite simple.

On April 26, 2012, Kiet Thanh Ly, a thirty-four-year-old homeless man born in Vietnam, purchased a knife from Smith's Marketplace near downtown Salt Lake City, and, at random, proceeded to attack the white men he came across in the parking lot. Two men that he succeeded in stabbing, Keltin Barney and Tim DeJulis, suffered near-life-threatening wounds: Keltin, stabbed nine times, survived a deep cut that went clean through his left arm and almost caused him to bleed to death; Tim endured a near-fatal blow to the head, resulting in severe brain trauma and significant memory loss. By chance, a man with a gun and a concealed-weapons permit named Doug Duncan appeared on the scene, drew his weapon, and told Ly to drop his knife and get on the ground. Doug had driven in from Idaho that day with his wife and two children to work with a television production crew for a supercross race being held in town; he happened to be standing behind Ly in the Smith's checkout line when Ly bought the knife. Doug remembers a disheveled-looking man in a dark coat fumbling with a plastic package, then the checkout clerk nervously telling him, just after selling Ly the knife, that she didn't "feel right" about Ly, that Doug and his family should "watch out for him" as they made their way out of the store.

As for Ly himself, I can tell you his height and eye color and the first time he shows up in the Salt Lake City police record. I know that he was born January 23, 1978, three years after the fall of Saigon in the country once known as South Vietnam. I know he was thirty-four years old at the time of the crime, that he was one of the many post-1975 Vietnamese refugees who came to the United States, eventually becoming a homeless drug addict who suffers from mental illness. Ly has lived the bulk of his peripatetic life in the Salt Lake Valley, disowned by family and largely forgotten by friends.

The facts I know about him are few and mostly related to his criminal record. According to court and police documents, since 1997 Ly has been charged with or convicted of a number of crimes, ranging from the petty to the violent, with other cases still pending; the charges include theft, drug possession, and an attempted assault on a police officer. I know that Ly was a patient at St. Mark's Hospital, a level-three trauma center near Mill Creek Canyon in Salt Lake, where he allegedly exposed himself to patients and hospital workers, and that his actions led to charges of sexual battery and lewdness. I know that in 2011, a year before his attack at Smith's, he was convicted on an amended charge of attempted aggravated assault for threatening an employee at the Department of Workforce Services with a knife. And I know that, only a week before he stabbed Keltin and Tim, Ly had been in jail on misdemeanor counts of joyriding and possessing someone else's ID.

Ly's case is, on its own terms, no mystery. There is no contention from any witness or published report that Ly did not commit these crimes, and though the system requires that defendants must first be judged competent to stand trial, there is evidence to suggest that Ly was, at the time of the stabbings, suffering from a psychotic break. Though startling, the crimes he committed are relatively minor by U.S. standards: only two people were injured, none fatally; the attacker was easily apprehended; the gun at the scene was not even fired. In our age of media immersion in gun violence, mass shootings, and terrorism, the stabbings at Smith's are a nonevent, the work of a homeless man with a history of mental illness and a meth addiction. But for me, Kiet Thanh Ly and the stabbings that took place at Smith's Marketplace, a superstore less than two miles from my home, have become an obsession likely to remain unresolved. Due to the severity of the mental health issues Ly suffers from, his lawyer, Tawni Hanseen, told me frankly on the phone that she wouldn't advise Ly or members of Ly's family to speak with me until the trial has finished. It goes without saying that Hanseen and the police won't answer my questions, either.

As a writer, I have no desire to interfere with the trial, and I certainly have no belief in Ly's innocence. My obsession with the case has less to do with Ly as a person and more to do with what he represents, his violent and ahistorical reimagining of his family's trauma, and our continued fascination with the Vietnam War. Mine is not a portrait of a crime, per se, but a snapshot of the effects of war on communities over time.

In revealing the effects of war over time, this crime is not simple, though the perpetrator is undisputed. The plain facts of this case conceal a compelling mystery. According to all newspaper accounts, throughout the stabbings Ly was heard to shout at passersby, "Why did you kill my people? You racist [expletive] . . . you killed my people, you should all die!" Though the parking lot was full of women, as well as men and teenagers of Chicano, Asian, and African descent, Ly specifically targeted white men near to his own age, telling police that the voice in his head insisted that these were the ones he needed to attack. At the pretrial, a young Japanese American man testified that Ly, rushing forward to stab him, stopped the moment he saw his face, spun around, and began running after people in the opposite direction. Eyewitnesses confirmed this, and many there that day said that they felt sure Ly's cries referred specifically to the Vietnam War, that he seemed to see his attack as some form of revenge.

But why would a man who had never personally experienced the Vietnam War suddenly need to act in response to it now? Why would he use this particular war as a reason for committing violence?

As I think over these questions, I don't know the city in which Ly was born, the names or ages of his siblings, or even if he has siblings. I don't know the exact route he traveled to America, whether he came to the United States through camps in Thailand, Malaysia, or the Philippines, or where his parents had worked and lived before they fled Vietnam. I don't know when he took his first drug, what need in him it satisfied. I know that he faces two felony counts of attempted murder and four counts of aggravated assault, and I also know that, to the courts and to those reading the newspaper, Ly isn't someone with a recognizable or sympathetic identity. Kiet Thanh Ly is a crime, one whose scale of destruction is relatively limited; until his trial is over, there's not much more anyone can learn about him, and little reason for the mainstream news media to pursue his story.

To write about Ly and violence is to write into a place of cultural speculation and possible fantasy: what I know or want to imagine about the Vietnam War and the experience of its refugees and their children, an experience I too easily and solely equate with war and with the past, though it is absurd to think that this is a war solely of the past, as we are still engaged in wars that regularly call upon the memory of Vietnam as both warning and criticism. Vietnam is the "bad war" we did not win, whose media-saturated shames we used to punish our returning veterans, the war we told ourselves not to emulate in Iraq and Afghanistan, the war to which we can't help but compare all other American wars. Ly's crime, his version of Vietnam, disappeared from the Salt Lake news cycle, but in the lives of many other Vietnamese refugees and refugees from other nations, some aspect of his story still lingers. Ly—the mentally ill refugee—is a figure of terror: the perpetual foreigner harboring his old, unfathomable grudges; a ticking time bomb of past traumas to be unleashed upon an unsuspecting host nation. Yet I suspect that labeling Ly insane in this way misses something crucial in our understanding of him, and the ways we imagine people like him, as well as our imaginative legacy of Vietnam. The case of Kiet Thanh Ly falls within that blurry area in which fact and imagination collide, and perhaps collude, with each other in creating a portrait of a war's long-term effects on us.

As this war's portraitist, I must reveal that my particular imagination was shaped by the manner in which I first learned of Ly's attack. At the time Keltin Barney and Tim DeJulis were fighting for their lives in the University of Utah hospital, I was living in Hanoi, two blocks away from the Ho Chi Minh Mausoleum and the Vietnam Military History Museum. I had read about their attack via a *Salt Lake Tribune* article link that a university colleague of mine who'd once had Keltin Barney as a student posted on Facebook.

But while I was horrified by what had happened to Keltin, I was also intrigued by Ly's cries. At the time of the crime, I had been living in Hanoi on a writing fellowship that required me to live outside North America for a year; I had chosen Hanoi for the sole reason that, though I had spent a lot of time living and traveling in Asia, I'd never been to Vietnam. Hanoi I'd chosen for similarly casual reasons: friends praised the city's pristine lakes and thriving art scene, its elegantly preserved French Quarter at the heart of the city near what seemed like a most auspicious monument for any writer to visit: the Temple of Literature.

But when I got to Hanoi, I discovered that the art scene had long ago followed the trail of money south, to Saigon. The city's narrow thoroughfares, once charmingly crowded with bicycles, were now choked by scooters and cars whose drivers refused to differentiate between sidewalk and street. The city's plentiful lakes were thick with plastic takeaway containers, used diapers, dog shit, rusted cans of soda and beer. Smog from traffic pollution hazed the city: anyone outside for long periods of time wore medical face masks or scarves of soft cotton pulled up tight to cover the nose and mouth. A thick, creamy scum, like the head on a pint of Guinness, coated the streams that ran through Trúc Bạch district, and the once-charming French Quarter had long ago turned into a grimy warren of shops catering to tourists and panhandlers.

Despondent, yet weirdly reluctant to change plans, I tried to make the best of the situation and moved to Ba Đình, also known as embassy row, just on the outskirts of the French Quarter. It was quieter there, and close to a number of parks that housed rows of ping-pong tables, infusing the area's nightlife with lively table-tennis tournaments and family outings. Hanoi was a thriving, high-traffic, industrial wasteland, where bookstores were as rare as birds outside of cages, friends difficult to make, and culture seemed to have been replaced with unbridled consumerism and intense black-market growth. The things that had attracted me to Hanoi had long ago disappeared, leaving me feeling irritated and faintly foolish about my decision and also, oddly, nostalgic for a city I had never known, and that likely had never existed.

The one thing I had not come to Hanoi to find, however, was war, much to the relief of the Vietnamese I met, who found the kind of "trauma tourism" that appealed to Westerners exhausting. "Oh, the war, the war, the *war*," groaned the writer Nguyen Qui Duc when another novel about postwar Vietnam came up in conversation. "As if all we were is *still* some third world war-torn country," gesturing to the busy road below his apartment: an avenue filled with cafés and shops, a bustling array of industries and needs. He was right: the war was long over and Hanoi was—for bad and good—rapidly globalizing. Duc himself seemed the perfect symbol of his country's hungry evolution: an elegant writer with white-streaked hair curling at his shoulders, he'd lived a number of years in San Francisco before returning to Hanoi to open up a seemingly endless number of dimly lit martini bars, each one disappearing as rapidly as it had appeared, only to be replaced by another, much like the beautiful and much younger women who appeared on his arm. Duc sighed as he glanced at me, one more American camped on his city's shifting periphery. "As if," he said, looking past me, "there was no other story to be told about Vietnam."

There are, of course, many other stories to be told about Vietnam. But the war was not a story I had known much about outside of history books, surprising as that may be for the daughter of a noncombat Air Force recruit during the Vietnam War and the niece of an Army soldier who'd received a Purple Heart for his service here. No one in my family spoke of the war: questions about my father's and uncle's service were neither expected nor, it seems, encouraged. War in my family meant silence, and over the years it gradually seemed rude to ask. And so it was with as much ignorance as curiosity that I visited the War Remnants Museum in Saigon to stare at images of children ravaged by Agent Orange; that I hunched under the low-hanging eaves of the "Hanoi Hilton" where John McCain had been tortured, peering at strange stains that bloomed on the walls; that I found myself near tears in the Vietnamese Women's Museum, reading about fourteen-year-old girls who'd served as some of the Viet Cong's most infamous leaders, and who—when caught—were viciously tortured.

But the monument that haunted me most was a sculpture composed of ruined plane parts heaped in the courtyard of the Vietnam Military History Museum. Just two blocks from my apartment, this sculpture—stacked to the height of a small house—took center stage in a courtyard filled with war's trophies: American Jeeps and Humvees, fighter planes, a series of tanks lined up in rows. Propped on a cement slab, the sculpture was a hulking mass of incongruous metals, scorched and dented and scarred, the planes' spoilers soldered into ailerons, wrenched-off bay doors tossed onto cockpits, windshields haphazarded with cracks. Planes from both the French and American wars had been composed into one twisted tower before which a giant black-and-white photo of a Viet Cong fighter had been propped. The fighter, a teenage girl, was dragging a piece of a plane wing with rope down the glassy sand of a beach.

The sculpture's meaning could not be clearer: even a young communist, in defense of her country, had power enough to bring down the militaries of most powerful countries on earth. It was an artwork of both propaganda and history, as all war monuments are, and yet something about these planes felt, the more I observed them, restless, enlarging. New emotions seemed to break through the sculpture's jingoistic crust, enlivening and contradicting its message. These planes were not representational figures made of stone and marble, as they might have been in a more sanitized monument that lined a capital's landscaped mall. They were *planes*. They were the real planes real men had died in, from which real men had killed other people. To look at these sheared-off wings was to be made intimately aware of war's mechanical, inhuman force. This monument was not triumphant, or perhaps I should say that this monument was not *only* triumphant: it both lamented and rejoiced in the deaths that made it, of which it made its audience materially aware.

The artwork was a sliver of war's terrible sublime, and perhaps it was the magnitude of the sensations that this piece aroused in me that made me suspect the sculptor had been duped by his creation or, better yet, had helped it slip the control of the politicians who commissioned it, men and women who wanted to tell only one story about the war, rather than the story the artist seemed to recognize. This was a sculpture that, even if unconsciously, elegized the deaths of Vietnam's enemies as much as it celebrated Hanoi's victors. I looked at this sculpture and saw inside its metal parts shapes that, rather like the emotions the work inspired, appeared to morph into strange new images emanating from the sheer enormity of the metal sculpture, menacing its spectators, radiating out through history. I saw some part of my father there, my uncle. I stood before the monument horrified, saddened, enraged.

Because I lived next door to the museum, I visited this sculpture frequently, taking notes, thinking that someday I would write something about it for myself, or that perhaps, alternately, I would come to this courtyard and sit by it and look at it and simply feel *less*. For a time, I visited the museum daily, believing that repeated exposure would numb these sensations that arose in the planes' presence, assure me that I had at last pinpointed the final sentiment behind the monument. I believed that, by articulating these sentiments for myself, I might encapsulate some idea central to understanding the war. But I never did.

It was during this period of time that I learned about Ly's stabbings. Something about his cry, "Why did you kill my people?" resonated with my visits to this sculpture, became an echo I could not get out of my head. My fascination with the memorial in Hanoi was also likely motivated by my fears and awareness of the wars we were still fighting, wars that I still associated with New York's Ground Zero site, which I visited in April 2002, months after the terrorist attacks of September 11, 2001. Alone, for one evening I walked the towers' razed perimeter, staring into their pit filled with piles of concrete and metal scaffolding, the site more like the blueprint for America's largest subterranean parking lot than a future memorial.

As in Hanoi, I'd stood transfixed by the site's enormity: its gaping, raw, yet mechanical maw, its chaotic interior of pipes and rebar hemmed in by a chain-link border. It was only after an hour that I noticed the young man: a dapper African American in a blue suit and well-cut wool coat. Smiling, he approached small groups of tourists standing by the fence and offered to walk them around the site, to explain what it was they were looking at. "Here," I watched him tell an older Japanese couple, "is where I heard the first plane hit the tower. That's where people jumped. And down that street, that's where I lived. I was eating breakfast right over there when I heard the first explosion, and then I started to run."

The Japanese couple, perhaps understanding him, perhaps not, followed him around the perimeter. I followed, too, listening as he went through every hour of his day, listing the avenues down which he ran, the friend's apartment he took shelter in, recalling—even as he smiled at the now-bewildered couple—the grit and stink of smoke he could not wash from his clothes. When he finished, the Japanese couple quietly thanked him and wandered on, while the young man moved off to find another group of tourists.

There was, I thought watching him, something both discomfiting and touching about this performance, a grief the young man repeated voluntarily—how many times per week? per day?—for the edification of strangers. It reminded me of a writer Keltin himself would reference when I spoke with him later of Ly's attack: Samuel Beckett, whose play *Krapp's Last Tape* features an old man who tries, and fails, to put to rest a memory from his youth that continues to haunt him. In the play, Krapp both recites and listens to his memories recorded onto different tapes, his memories spooling and spooling, though he finds within them no closure. Surely, at some point in his life, the man will find the right words, the tapes will finish, the memory will be complete. But the tapes are never finished. They are always being rewound, replayed, revised. The play is a study in both memory and time, about the repetitive losses none of us can escape. In the end, we are haunted by the stories we keep alive in our consciousness because we cannot or will not find the words to put them to rest, compelled to resuscitate events we cannot articulate or comprehend.

I followed the smattering of articles that emerged that week about Ly and Keltin and Tim with interest, stopping only when the articles themselves dried up. I forgot the case, or half remembered it. When I returned to the States months later, Keltin's name came up in conversation. I Googled the case to learn its outcome. To my surprise, the case was still pending. And more than three years later, as I began to look for answers about the crime, it still was.

3 Whenever I mention Ly's crime to friends outside of Utah, the first shock they express is not about the stabbing, but about the fact that there are Vietnamese in Utah. In fact, the Vietnamese community is one of the fastest-growing groups in the Salt Lake Valley, though it is nowhere near the size of the communities found in Houston, Los Angeles, and around Washington, D.C. The enduring image and fact of Salt Lake City's predominant whiteness, however, is one of the reasons the U.S. government wanted to send post-1975 Vietnamese refugees here to begin with: to break up potential "ethnic enclaves" they feared would take root. After the fall of Saigon, the government wanted to assimilate the flood of Southeast Asians into American life as quickly as possible, and so it scattered families around small towns across America, in areas where they would almost assuredly be the only Asians. Salt Lake was, and continues to be, one of the most popular refugee relocation sites in the States. Now there are around ten thousand Vietnamese living in Salt Lake, as compared to 1.9 million nationally. Still, as an ethnic minority, this is a significant community by Salt Lake standards, constituting roughly 1 percent of the valley's total population. The community is also small enough that most Vietnamese families are in some contact with each other, which is how I was able to piece together parts of Ly's life, when requests to speak with his ex-girlfriend and family were rebuffed.

Ly is one of the more than nine hundred thousand refugees from Vietnam, Laos, and Cambodia who settled in the United States between 1975 and 1990 after having been uprooted by continuing military conflicts. Though Vietnam's war with America ended in

1975, Vietnam's long period of fighting with the Khmer Rouge in Cambodia began soon after, as did China's invasion of North Vietnam in 1979 and the Communist Party's internal witch hunt for former South Vietnamese sympathizers. After the North Vietnamese take-over, more than a million people were sent to re-education camps, while the government worked to dismantle the private businesses of the Hoa, ethnic Chinese living in and around Saigon who formed the backbone of South Vietnam's capitalist trade. Vietnam post-1975 was rife with domestic and international conflicts waged simulta-neously: for many former South Vietnamese citizens, to stay in this new nation meant to fight the Khmer Rouge and possibly be killed; to be sent to re-education camps and have your family destroyed; or to keep your head down, pay off local police and officials, and eke out whatever living you could.

The first refugees to the United States are distinguished by their relative privilege: this first wave of roughly one hundred thirty thousand Vietnamese was more educated, wealthier, and better connected, often tied to the U.S. embassy or military. Thus, the first wave's relocation and, to some extent, migration experiences were more positive. The second wave of Vietnamese, who fled between 1978 and the mid-1980s, however, struggled. Commonly called "boat people," this group included the less-educated Hmong tribespeople uprooted from along the Cambodian border in Laos who were now fleeing the Khmer Rouge. The bulk of the relocating Vietnamese, however, were Hoa who were fleeing Communist persecution or who had been encouraged to leave by the government—after paying a fee of several thousand dollars. The third and final wave of refugees in the late 1980s and early 1990s was largely composed of Amerasians and political prisoners released from re-education camps, struggling to make their way abroad to reconnect with family.

Escape was fraught with the very real danger of being caught by police, who closely monitored the movement of people in villages, particularly the children of former South Vietnamese soldiers and

U.S. sympathizers. Capture meant prison, re-education camps, or conscription into the army, especially for the sons of former South Vietnamese servicemen. Officers who'd fought for the South could be rounded up and sent to camps, where they would be interrogated and tortured: one woman told me that her father had been held for three years, during which time her mother had traveled from camp to camp trying to locate him, her luggage laden with rotting care packages. Boys could be forced to work patrol units along the Cambodian border, where they might be killed in skirmishes with the Khmer Rouge, while girls were targeted by local police for re-education camps. Parents wanting to protect their children could be bled dry by bribes paid to officials. Many felt that a better, if not safer, option was to ferry your family out of the country under cover of night.

Those who chose this option paid financially crippling bribes to the government and to fishermen—"Vietnamese coyotes," one interviewee I spoke with called them—who smuggled them out on junks and trawlers to Thailand, Malaysia, and the Philippines, where families had to wait to find sponsorship, languishing for up to a year in makeshift camps, sometimes even broken up so that individual family members could be relocated to different states and nations. But the ones who made it out of the camps were lucky. The flood of refugees strained local Southeast Asian economies and infuriated officials, who argued that their nations didn't have the infrastructure to support such a rapid influx of people. Each month brought refugees out in the tens of thousands: in June 1979 alone, nearly fifty-four thousand people flooded onto foreign shores, the number dropping only when the United States pledged to accept fourteen thousand refugees per month indefinitely, in response to Hanoi's promise to curtail the flow out of the country. Until then, nations sent coast guard ships out to intercept boats before they landed, sometimes forcing them back out to sea for weeks or even months until they could find a place to land, or were rescued by passing freighters. Because large vessels were easier to spot, to avoid capture, refugees sought out fishing boats as small as twenty feet. But small boats were never intended for navigating open water, and so thousands died at sea, capsizing in storms or preyed upon by pirate vessels that sought them out, stripping refugees of gold and cash, raping or abducting girls and women, occasionally killing all aboard by ramming the boat repeatedly until it sank.

The exact number of people who died during flight remains a mystery, but the United Nations High Commissioner for Refugees estimates that between 1978 and 1990, some eight hundred and forty thousand refugees successfully fled Vietnam by boat, while around two hundred and fifty thousand others were lost at sea. Stories of being adrift for weeks, of starvation, theft, rape, and murder, rumors even of cannibalism filter through many families. These traumatic tales of flight are hidden from or recounted to children and grandchildren alike, either to protect them from the horrors of the past, or to justify their parents' strict discipline, the anxious expectations they nurture for their children's success.

To outsiders, the Vietnamese who resettled in the United States look like a success story continually in the making: the war-spawned cracks that fissure their community are pasted over with media tales of thriving nail salons and white-collar aspirations. But this sunny media image belies the complex class, regional, and ethnic differences that play out within Vietnamese American social life in cities all across the nation. Even a small community like the one in Salt Lake is a complex mélange of immigrant and refugee, rich and poor, urban and tribal, Southern and Northern, ex-soldier and noncombatant alike. In the late 1970s and early 1980s, when families like Ly's arrived—late second-wave "boat people"—Utah offered almost no refugee support: state public assistance services that included language and occupational training had been shut down months after the first wave arrived. Of the twelve thousand Southeast Asian refugees who arrived in Utah just after 1975, around half found employment on production lines, or doing other manual labor. Thus, refugees assimilated not through education but through blue-collar work—yet their children and grandchildren would graduate high school and attend local community colleges and universities, so families in the valley thus experienced sharp divides between generations, not only in terms of educational opportunities, but in terms of class mobility.

The Vietnamese American community in Salt Lake is described by its members as divisive, materialistic, conformist, even classist. While the community isn't large enough for the luxury of deep ideological divides, its lack of a cohesive structure is, in itself, the product of war, as some people I interviewed told me, and the class, political, and ethnic conflicts in Utah replicate those from their original homeland. For example, owners of a popular restaurant who hail from the North regularly switch to a different dialect of Vietnamese when serving customers from the South, in order to mask their origins and potentially woo a larger clientele. In general, the Vietnamese who fled Vietnam post-war nurse staunchly anti-Communist sympathies, and differences in political opinion are not tolerated. The community is socially conservative, and recent Vietnamese immigrants from northern Vietnam are looked upon with suspicion, even derision.

The Lys originally lived in South Vietnam, but other than that, they would have suffered from nearly all other class and political comparisons in Salt Lake. Poorer, and with less education, the Lys were second-wave boat people who struggled to get by in the United States, living paycheck to paycheck, according to friends. Within and outside the family, there was no support for someone suffering from drug addiction and mental illness, so Ly likely would have found himself ostracized or ignored, seen as a figure of shame. The Vietnamese American community does not dwell on its failures. If Ly was invisible to the state of Utah until he entered its criminal justice system, he would have been equally invisible to his community, a person other Vietnamese Americans would have wanted to avoid, part of a painful past—and a hopeless future—that everyone wanted to jettison.

Freudian psychoanalysis theorizes trauma as a double blow, the first of such psychic force that the shock never entirely registers in the victim's consciousness. This first blow is followed by a period of latency, after which new symptoms surface, breaking through the crust of consciousness. Because the first blow has been so deeply repressed, however, sometimes to the point of erasing the first memory entirely, these secondary traumas register more powerfully than the first. Now this second trauma is the only one you can remember. You've forgotten the first blow, you've denied it, and the shock you feel anew has broken through your memory's understanding and experience of time, shattering the past into the present, disrupting your ability to remember history without reliving it.

Trauma induces fear, horror, a sense of helplessness. Post-traumatic stress disorder (PTSD), an anxiety disorder that can follow traumatic events, forces the traumatized person to re-experience these emotions in an endlessly repeating loop. PTSD occurs when the physical response to trauma becomes the body's default setting, or a setting accessed easily even under normal, nontraumatic conditions. Startle a person with PTSD, and he sweats, his mind races, his heart pounds. He feels terrified as if under siege while his amygdala—the part of the brain that releases emotions associated with memories—shoots back and forth in time, bathing the brain with stress-related hormones. The body floods with adrenaline, under-regulating the immune system to such an extent that over time, the body becomes more vulnerable to the inflammation associated with chronic diseases such as arthritis, diabetes, and cardiovascular disease.

Reading about the experiences of refugees might make one believe that these communities have experienced levels of trauma that would make war and relocation seem like ever-continuous threats: the whole community, in that sense, may be characterized as at risk of developing PTSD. This is, naturally, something Southeast Asian refugees have resisted, not wanting to be seen as pathologized by their history. But trauma and its effects on the Vietnamese community have been well studied, and the general picture suggests there is a connection that can't be ignored. Currently, Vietnamese Americans who arrived in the United States as political refugees suffer from higher rates of mental health issues; those over fifty-five were found by researchers for a University of California, Irvine, Center for Health Care Management and Policy study to be twice as likely as whites to report needing mental health care. Asian American communities notoriously underreport mental health problems, because of the stigma they attach to mental illness services and also language barriers, but the study revealed that Vietnamese Americans were substantially more likely than other Asian Americans to seek help from mental health services, most likely because of the traumas they experienced before and after fleeing Vietnam.

The immigrant population in general, however, has much lower rates of mental health issues than refugees, and in some cases immigrants prove better adjusted than natives of the host country. In a 2011 article published in the *Canadian Medical Association Journal*, researchers reviewed the prevalence of mental disorders in all immigrants to Canada and found that the overall rates were slightly *lower* than those of the general Canadian-born population, and that newly arrived immigrants (those who have lived in their adoptive country for less than four years) had lower rates of depression, anxiety, or alcohol dependence than the Canadian-born population. Once the Vietnamese immigrant had established a home in Canada, however, the rate of disorders rose as immigrants' health worsened, usually to match that of the Canadian-born population. Rates of disorders in immigrants also varied by region: of the immigrant populations surveyed, the ones with the highest rates of mental disorders were from Europe, the lowest from Africa and Asia.

In general, refugees are at a higher risk for developing mental health disorders such as PTSD, depression, chronic pain, and other somatic problems. Exposure to war, violence, torture, rape, forced migration and exile, financial upheaval, and uncertain legal status: all these factors mean refugees can suffer from elevated levels of psychiatric disorders, even at up to ten times the rate of members of the general population.

Article after article suggests that members of the Vietnamese diaspora, which includes refugees and nonrefugee immigrants, is in general at a higher risk for anxiety, depression, and some other mental illnesses, and that these problems follow wherever Vietnamese communities have taken root. Problems for refugees, however, are particularly acute. One Norwegian study tracked a number of its refugees since their initial relocation to Norway, and found that, though the mental health of the refugees as a whole had improved significantly since their arrival, their mean scores on mental distress tests remained elevated: almost a fifth of the sampled population— more than twice the percentage of native-born Norwegians—had higher psychological distress scores, suggesting that even over time, Vietnamese refugees remained vulnerable.

The Vietnamese are one of the few groups with enough longitudinal data to give us a picture of the long-term costs associated with relocation. Currently, the world is undergoing the worst global refugee crisis in generations: as of June 2015, there were 16.7 million refugees in foreign countries worldwide, most of them uprooted by conflicts in Syria, Iraq, Ukraine, and Afghanistan. At the same time, extreme poverty and climate problems continue to push thousands out of parts of sub-Saharan Africa and Southeast Asia. It is tempting to apply what we know about the mental well-being of postdiaspora Vietnamese to these incoming groups, to predict that the children of these wars will follow the same pattern. However, when the United States began accepting what would become nearly a million Vietnamese refugees in total, it had no long-term infrastructure in place. State-assisted programs for language and occupational training offered support lasting a few months at best, sometimes sponsoring refugees for as little as a few weeks: refugees were largely left to their own devices to learn English, to find work, to adapt to their new homes. Similarly, health organizations were not trained to deal with the challenges a multilingual Southeast Asian population presented. The weakness of these crucial support structures meant that the mental health needs of the most vulnerable people in these communities were never addressed, and, in part because of insufficient care, the conditions of these suffering individuals often worsened.

However, although reported rates of mental health issues in refugee populations remain elevated, the majority of the Vietnamese American community does not appear to display symptoms of PTSD. One reason we may believe that PTSD must be universal for Vietnamese refugees stems from our imagining of the Vietnam War itself, which has provided us with a popular narrative for returning veterans and refugees alike. Studies indicate that PTSD rates and symptoms are equivalent across veteran and refugee cultures. If this is true, it's good to look at the numbers. The recent National Vietnam Veterans Longitudinal Study reveals that, forty years after the Vietnam War, from 70 to 75 percent of veterans studied have never shown any mental illness linked to war, whether PTSD, depression, or drug or alcohol addiction. In many ways then, the real story about Vietnam and its veterans and refugees is one of resilience, not trauma.

According to David J. Morris, author of *The Evil Hours*, our tendency to exaggerate the trauma associated with the war reveals how we much have pathologized war in general, along with the veteran's experience. No longer do we imagine that war can be cathartic, a rite of passage for the young, a necessary test that allows young men to bond or prove their physical prowess. It is unfashionable, even barbaric, to suggest that any aspect of war might be good for a young person to experience. A large part of this is due to our memory of the catastrophic conflicts that defined the nineteenth and twentieth centuries: from the Civil War to Iraq, the American image of war has been constructed on the belief that war solely devastates, and this belief has weakened or strengthened depending on the political popularity of the war at hand. It is easy to applaud the efforts of World War II veterans, but Vietnam, Korea, Iraq, and Afghanistan all changed our notions about the nobility of combat and brought into popular usage a whole new vocabulary to describe wartime experience, giving rise to terms like PTSD, and to the belief that entire communities might be traumatized. With Vietnam, war and trauma became synonymous. In this way, the Vietnam War radically shifted our thinking about the politics of combat. From literature and film to political speeches, from antiwar activism to the growing veterans' movement, everything in the American media has responded to the change. The consensus is clear: Vietnam created an entirely different breed of refugee and veteran.

4 Keven Lee sits across from me in the South Jordan Beans & Brews, watching me nervously inhale a giant sausage roll. He is here as a favor to a mutual Facebook friend who knows about my interest in the Vietnamese American community. Cheryl, a doctor who works on the west side of Salt Lake with many Vietnamese American patients, connected us. I am not, by nature, the kind of person who enjoys badgering a stranger into telling me his life story. Still, here we are. Keven, it turns out, knows the Lys socially, and I have invited myself into Keven's life so as to piece together the thoughts of a man some might say at the moment of his attack *had* no conscious thoughts.

Here is Keven's initial assessment of Ly: "Kiet came to the U.S. with his parents and two brothers," Keven tells me now, "but he was just a normal young boy. I don't know any reason why he turned into this; the only thing I can think of is drugs. We go out to eat and I see him talking to himself. I think if anything is twisted in his head, it's due to the drugs, not the war."

Keven is stocky, dark skinned. He's wearing a pressed pink polo shirt and crisply ironed shorts. Born to a well-to-do family in Ho Chi Minh City, formerly Saigon, he moved to Provo in 1990 with his parents, brother, and sister when he was fifteen. Earlier, during the war, his mother worked for the U.S. embassy in Saigon, while his father taught Vietnamese at a local school. His maternal uncle, a pilot for the U.S. government, was in the first group airlifted out of the country; this same uncle later helped Keven's family find a U.S. sponsor.

Keven is aware of what his country symbolizes to people like me: violence and war, dislocation, grief. He understands that the popular narrative of who he must be is, in some ways, tied to trauma, though his own story, Keven insists, is one of healing, not violence. The insidious popularity of the traumatized-refugee story means that Keven spends our afternoon carefully choosing his words when talking about Ly. I am struck by how strenuously he criticizes him. It's the drug use, he insists. It's his bad choice of friends or it's his interest in crime, meaning that to Keven, Ly has consciously decided to fail. I suspect that it distances Keven from being seen as like Ly, and from the possibility of any social or physical breakdown on his own part; it denies that there is something about his own relocation he couldn't control. Keven cannot afford to be nostalgic about a country he barely knows, I understand; part of being the successfully assimilated citizen means appearing, to strangers like me, entirely unconflicted about your life. 29

As for his parents, whatever traumas they suffered, Keven insists, came not from war or relocation, but from the long and sometimes failed process of assimilation. Keven's family was trained for six months in the culture of their future home while waiting in a refugee camp in the Philippines, but their ESL classes taught them only basic expressions: "Hello," "Goodbye," "How much does this cost?" None of these lessons prepared them for Provo, the high-altitude home of Brigham Young University and winters that can last up to six months. Upon their arrival, since they were clad in thin, second-hand clothing bought for them at Deseret Industries, the cold hit Keven and his family like a slap. For the first few weeks, they wandered through their lives in hazy disbelief, shocked by the snow, by the blocky, painful consonants of English, by the fact that everyone seemed underdressed, fleshy and melon pale in the dead of winter. Everything looked enormous to Keven—the cars, streets, the people—and eerily clean. His breakfasts tasted like ash, the cheese in his lunch sandwiches smelled rancid. Keven's family had been sponsored by a white LDS family with whom he and his parents struggled to communicate: at night, he'd lie awake hungry, afraid to ask for something to eat. His father, meanwhile, snuck into the bathroom to smoke cigarettes so as not to offend his Mormon sponsors. But one day the bathroom fan broke, and smoke wafted out into the narrow hall. The host father, furious, yelled at him. Keven's father stood erect while listening, his head bowed. The next day, out of shame, he quit smoking cold turkey.

Keven found himself alone everywhere he went: at school, at stores, in the LDS church his parents made Keven join as a way of thanking their Mormon sponsors. Keven also found himself constantly starving—school lunch was something else it took months to learn about and ask for—and frustrated to discover that the other young Asians in his school spoke only English. After classes, he'd walk home to meet his siblings, the only other Vietnamese in the area. Three years later, after his sophomore year in high school, his parents moved to South Jordan to join a Vietnamese community, and Keven, for the first time since his arrival, found himself friends.

But while Keven has found a way, slowly, to adapt, Keven's parents continue to feel lost in their adoptive country. It's different for them here, Keven insists, and though his own identity has been built on the shaky ground of ever-shifting loyalties, he knows his parents see themselves as rooted in Vietnam. Still, they are not like the group of ex–South Vietnamese soldiers who get drunk at parties, meeting every month to reminisce about the war and home. His parents have no illusions about what they left or why: they are happy here, they insist. They are becoming happy. "This country," Keven repeats to me over the hour, "is heaven compared to where we came from."

For Keven to say that his parents remain "rooted in Vietnam" is, for me, an interesting phrase. The Vietnam that Keven's parents lost is of course different from the Vietnam that Keven lost. When Keven and Ly fled Vietnam, they left a country they'd been taught since birth not to consider their real home. Their homeland, according to their parents, would always be South Vietnam: the now-imaginary nation shimmering beneath the political facade of the country they went to school in, made friends in, walked in, lived in. Their true country did and did not exist, its borders animated and maintained by their parents' memories.

And now in America, this Vietnam has again been changed by our popular imagination into a place of continual war: in that sense, Keven's country has been lost a third time. Keven must struggle to articulate a national identity he is never entirely allowed to possess: his Vietnam is always in opposition to his parents' or an outsider's Vietnam. In this way, his Vietnam does and does not exist, since it constantly changes depending on the person with whom he speaks. It isn't the past that makes you crazy, Keven suggests, it isn't even a war or fleeing it. It's the stories that come from inside of and out-side of your community, enforcing this sense that you've escaped a place that can only be accessed through someone else's imagination. There is no return to that nation except through fantasy or narra-tive, through metaphors constructed by someone else. In that sense, Vietnam has become what any country famous for a war becomes: a hybrid of memorial and nation.

It is why, I think, Keven has become obsessed with the absence of another conventional symbol he could rely on: a flag that he might display in his house. Should he choose the green and gold flag of his parents' South Vietnam, he asks, or the red and gold-starred flag of the current country? It is only a small problem, he starts to tell me, but then changes his mind. It is not a small problem. It grows bigger each year, worsening as his children age. If he takes up his parents' flag, his friends will see it as a willful anachronism, but the current flag only makes him seem pro-communist, a slap in the face to his parents and his uncle who fought in the war.

Of course, he could hang the American flag, but something about this feels wrong to him, or like a concession: it would be something he's chosen, not something he is. Keven wants an image that's been culturally preconstructed for him, a symbol with an identity that he can slip inside of, as others have slipped inside it: something as small as a flag, and just as monumental.

"I was born in a country that no longer exists," Bhanu Kapil writes in *Schizophrene*, a book of poems that examines the intersection between mental illness and migration in the post-partition South Asian diaspora. Kapil's statement reminds me that the act of crossing borders is as much a spiritual as a physical process, one that disorders the migrant and her very sense of imagining the world: when a nation's borders have been historically dissolved as well as crossed, the migrant must see some part of herself as both perpetually and fundamentally deracinated. It is not the immediate shock of confronting a new culture, but the generational eroding of self and memory that most destabilizes; it is, as Kapil suggests, the voices of a past that cannot ever be assimilated into the present that permanently wound, so that the body of the migrant becomes a hybrid country, one inhabited by her parents' ghosts.

Keven, when I suggest this reading to him, agrees. This sense of being fundamentally nationless has haunted both him and Ly; it has confused many other members of their community, especially those born after 1975. Keven talks to people about it often, asking friends at parties what flag they would buy, what symbol from this lost nation they might wear. "And 99 percent of them say the same thing," he tells me. "They don't have one. They're confused. Everyone's confused. I think it was confusing for Kiet, too." And the end result of all this confusion, he realizes, is the lingering sense that people like him, and people like Ly, don't really live anywhere.

"Confusion," Keven says, and what he means is both the physical world that he and his parents entered when they stepped off the plane into Utah from subtropical Manila, and also the psychic anxieties of living on another culture's margins. Nearly thirty years after their repatriation, his mother still dislikes leaving home, preferring to stay indoors with her husband, watching a continuous stream of

Vietnamese videos. Keven's parents do not go to restaurants that aren't Vietnamese. They don't open their doors to strangers, and they avoid at all costs the police. They are not unlike the mothers and fathers and grandparents of dozens of people Keven knows, some less or more hampered by their lack of English, their constant sense of uneasiness, by the awareness they have no other escape route or home. They sense that their origins make them both invisible and inferior to the predominant culture, and their decades-long struggles—and failures—to succeed according to the image of the model minority fill them with both frustration and shame.

Describing them, Keven grows animated. "Crazy," he tells me, is the definition of someone who can't make friends with his neighbor because he lacks confidence and language. It is the mother shaking in the aisles of the grocery store because she can't figure out what all the food costs, the uncle who hesitates to drive because he's afraid of the signs and the cops. What is crazy, he asks, but the pent-up terrors that compose this daily foreign life? "Crazy," Keven finishes, "is just a term to explain something that doesn't make sense to you."

Keven spreads his hands on the table. He's agitated now, his voice rising and rising as he speaks. "I feel crazy, too," he says, "Kiet and I, we came to the United States about the same time, and I know who he is and how he is, so I see my story in his. Because even though you know me for years, you don't know who I am. I could snap the next day. I could go like that," he says, and smacks his hands loudly against the table. At the sudden noise, the tables behind us look up. A white mother and child, a white couple sharing a sandwich. Aware that he has unsettled our neighbors, Keven flushes, and stops. He hides his hands beneath the table.

My uncle, my mother's brother, received the Purple Heart and a Bronze Star for his service in Vietnam. My uncle is Chinese American; in the past, I often wondered what it must have been like to fight and almost die with troops trying to kill people who looked, physically, just like him, among soldiers who might even have viewed his presence with suspicion. The poet Yusef Komunyakaa, an African American who fought in Vietnam, writes explicitly about this, about the costs of fighting for a nation that doesn't recognize all its soldiers as its own. In his prose poem "The One-Legged Stool," Komunyakaa imagines a black GI, captured by the Viet Cong, arguing over the loyalty his fellow white troops will show him, insisting, "They ain't laughing [at me]. Ain't cooperating [with you]. It ain't the way you say it is. I'm American." The black soldier refuses to accept what the Viet Cong whisper: that Martin Luther King has been assassinated, that the white troops have sold him out. He rails against the Viet Cong's terrifying logic: loyalty like the black GI's is insane. Despite what he suspects, he clings to his identity as a soldier, the symbol of his uniform so protective "you could cut your fingers on the creases in [his] khakis." "I didn't break," he insists, regardless of the fact that he already has been, fighting for a country that even its enemies know hasn't granted him full humanity.

My uncle fought in Vietnam twenty years after Truman integrated the armed forces, twenty-six years after Japanese Americans were interned in camps even as the Japanese American 442nd Infantry Regiment helped liberate Dachau. He was wounded three years after the 1965 Immigration Act, which allowed the first big wave of

Chinese and other Asian immigrants into America after years of draconian race-based restrictions, and he was still recuperating from the war in 1969, the same year Hoover testified before the Senate that China was flooding the United States with communist propaganda along with refugees and immigrants, and that among the many hundreds of thousands of Chinese living in the States were dozens of subversives ready to sabotage the nation.

In Vietnam, my uncle would have been implicitly asked to set aside his Chinese American racial identity to become a working cog in a military that would represent his interests as a U.S. citizen, even while the nation diminished him as an Asian man. Was it the first time he understood the cost of what it meant to be Chinese American? I wanted to know, but there is something about my uncle, a quiet dignity, a wry sense of self-deprecating humor, that would make asking such questions impossible. His service was known by all of us in the family but never discussed: until recently, never in my life had I heard my uncle mention his time in the Army. From conversations with my father, I learned that my uncle spent most of his tour stationed on a mountain ridge that the Viet Cong air force shelled almost nightly. According to my father, the combat my uncle endured was brutal, relentless. Only in the summer of 2016, at our family reunion, did my uncle speak explicitly about his service, and that was to say that he'd finally put that time in his life to rest. From this, I understood we shouldn't expect to hear anything more from him. My mother, when my uncle's health problems come up—he suffers from trembling, sudden fainting spells, memory loss, and heart palpitations no doctor seems able to explain—will darkly allude to Agent Orange, but none of us knows. And it is not because none of us cares, but because none of us can imagine how to parse that word *Vietnam*, which, in our house, has turned into a metaphor for both silence and the costs of a potentially suicidal loyalty.

The fact that Ly attacked only white men in the Smith's parking lot as revenge for Vietnam makes little sense, considering the racial makeup of the U.S. armed services that fought in Southeast Asia, though it is consistent with his disturbed appropriation of the war and its aftershocks. In that context, whiteness matters. When the Vietnamese who were repatriated in Utah were sent to overwhelmingly white and LDS towns along the Wasatch Front, or to the Hispanic neighborhoods on the east bench of Salt Lake, this attempt to speed up their assimilation could also have looked like an attempt to culturally cripple them. Certainly, the cultural differences must have proved too dramatic for some: after only a few years in Utah, less than half the refugees decided to remain, moving on in search of larger Asian communities in California, Texas, and on the East Coast.

Whiteness can have corrosive effects on nonwhite populations, slowly eroding people's sense of self through the shame of cultural judgment in which everything they know—their language, food, family, even their sense of what is and is not attractive—must be reappraised through new norms. Faced with this reality—of having to construct an identity built in response to someone else's curiosity or prejudice—some begin to feel as if they have no concrete foundation at all.

"Racial melancholia" is a concept literary scholars employ to describe this phenomenon. The concept draws on Freud's *Mourning and Melancholia*, which describes a response to loss that becomes pathological when the melancholic refuses to stop grieving the lost object or ideal, and instead incorporates this loss into his sense of self. By refusing to finish mourning, the melancholic haunts himself, identifying with the object of his loss to such an extent that he cannot separate his ego from the object or his grief. Over the past century, Freud's theory has been expanded to include the psychology of gays and lesbians, people of color, postcolonial subjects: any group which might identify itself not just through a particular set of physical traits or cultural bonds, but through a collective memory of unresolved injury and loss.

"Racial melancholia" specifically refers to the ways that cultural assimilation devalues a nonwhite person's sense of self. In a society where nonwhite attributes and cultures are disparaged, where whiteness is an ideal that can never be universally attained, people of color are implicitly compelled to identify with negative portrayals or images. To try and counteract these stereotypes may lead a person to fixate on them, trying to remake herself into the unattainable ideal. American assimilation—with its goal of refashioning immigrants according to Protestant, white, masculine, and heterosexual values—capitalizes on this process, in which the ideal of whiteness is continually lost and continually mourned, encouraging a cycle of self-erasure that, as with Ralph Ellison's famously nameless protagonist, ensures invisibility.

When I read about Ly's case, some part of me saw his crime as a brutal way to counteract that invisibility, to kill the ideal that he could never achieve, and that had, consciously or not, kept him on the outskirts of a culture he couldn't join. In this, he reminded me of the soldier in Komunyakaa's poem, of his fellow troops' suspicion that within any non-white body lurks a traitor to be teased out, one constantly being asked to choose between conflicting identities. Any refugee or immigrant knows of this suspicion: it is why she struggles so hard to contradict these narratives, embracing—sometimes too enthusiastically—the cultural markers that make her appear assimilated.

I am familiar with this narrative. As a half-Chinese and half-white woman, I've grown up surrounded by pictures of white bodies I could never completely mirror, and surrounded, too, by images of idealized Asian girls whose resemblance in either temperament or body to my own mother or cousins or grandmother was negligible. My grandmother had stopped speaking Chinese as an attempt to assimilate us; while she preferred I date Chinese boys, she also seemed to sense that my white appearance might be a benefit, and so she praised my light hair, she told me I must be popular at school. It was not that

I didn't consider Asian women pretty; I had cousins with black hair and tall, athletic figures who crowded together at parties, coolly distant. I envied them, and felt that, next to them, whatever Asianness I possessed was somehow lesser. But the Asian woman the media admired was a kind of fantasy I had no experience with or interest in. The Asian woman I knew was neither docile nor girlish. She was the mother whose appearance I'd heard mocked by kids at my white private school, whose PhD was erased by the white stranger whose car collided with hers and who, while asking for her insurance information, spoke pidgin because he didn't believe she could speak English. As for myself, I studied the habits and clothing styles of older white kids, enviously trying to ape the little tics that would let me blend in. I learned to fetishize my ability to disappear; at the same time, I seethed at this invisibility. In college, I plucked my eyebrows—thick as paintbrush strokes, as my mother had called them—down to the thin arched lines I saw on white actresses' faces. To my dismay, they have never grown back. I have cosmetically erased one of my most defining Asian features, rendering me—even to myself when I look at pictures taken of me as a child—unrecognizable.

If being white is impossible, Trinh Mai thought to herself as a child, *then at least I can pass as Mexican.* This, at least, is the gist of what she tells me over lunch during our talk. Trinh is a University of Utah social work professor I met through mutual friends and colleagues. Unlike Keven or Ly, Trinh did not come to Utah as a child, but spent her childhood in Poteet, Texas, a town of around three thousand people, most of them Chicano. For Trinh, *American* meant a mix of white and mostly Mexican American culture: only with the Chicano kids at school could she relax, she says, watching them, like her, navigate between languages, her own English at first limited to the words "girl," "boy," and "table." Less than a week after leaving her refugee camp, Trinh was dropped off with her family at a Texas reassignment center, where she spent the day gorging on ice cream.

The next day she was woken early, before the sun even rose, to make the long drive to her first American school. There she spent the day with an assigned "best friend" in the front row of class, staring at the teacher, feeling faintly electrified. At recess, she stood with her back pressed tightly against the school's brick wall, surrounded by children, their mouths opening and closing at her like fish.

Trinh and her immediate family were the only Vietnamese in Poteet, and so Trinh spent no time with other children like herself. When Trinh attended high school years later in Houston, she found other Vietnamese Americans, but she avoided them, having heard from her friends that Asians were the nerds she should ignore. At school, her appearance allowed her to blend in with her Mexican friends; at home, however, she slipped back into the culture she'd learned never to speak about, arguing in Vietnamese with her mother, sleeping in her grandmother's bedroom. It wasn't until college, when she met other Asian Americans who had similar stories, that she understood the reason that she'd repressed her family's past for so long: after Trinh's parents settled in Texas, her father developed full-blown schizophrenia.

Trinh's father was the eldest son of a once-prosperous businessman who had frittered money away on poor trade decisions and gambling debts: it was Trinh's grandmother who'd saved their family from poverty by opening up a sewing business, all the while lavishing attention upon Trinh's socially anxious father. Throughout his adolescence, Trinh's father hated guests and avoided strangers. *The family scholar*, they called him, to excuse the ways he hid in his room when company came over.

During the war, his anxiety worsened, ripening into schizophrenia after the family's relocation to Texas. Trinh recalls a man who seemed to drift through life, dozing on the living room sofa, drugged with psychotropics, his semiconscious haze not unlike the dementia suffered by Trinh's elderly grandfather, who had relocated with them. Growing up, Trinh saw her home carefully maintained by women but filled with disabled men—a situation she thinks her younger brother has taken to heart. It has made him passive, she says, isolated, and, like their father, socially anxious. Her brother has few friends, Trinh says, and at age thirty-five is still financially supported by their mother. Trinh worries about him, and worries, too, that his anxiety might be a quieter, lengthier form of self-harm.

As she talks about her brother, Trinh's voice grows quiet. Trinh, like Keven before her, began our conversation by denying that wartime trauma played any part in her family life, but when we speak about her father and her brother, she cannot ignore the possibility that both men were scarred by war. Or that, if war did not directly wound them, it awakened something dormant in them. Trinh pauses, looking pained as she talks about her brother, and I realize I am asking her to discuss something almost too raw for her to process. I am asking her to talk about shame. This is the subject hovering inside of and around our conversation: the sense that even as a child Trinh suspected her father and brother were too broken to survive, that her family might be seen by strangers as deficient. Were I to be honest in turn, I would admit to the cousin and the great uncles in the Chinese half of my own family who had long ago retreated to their bedrooms or to alcohol, wasting away days with video games. Shame is something we protect ourselves and loved ones from, if we can, and there may be a special shame on behalf of men who are vulnerable, whether due to illness, money, or injury: a weakness only compounded by racial difference. To admit a weakness like this exists in your family feels like a double failure: a betrayal of these men's confidence, and an admission of your own potential unassimilability.

And yet shame suffuses the narratives of both relocation and repatriation: for refugees and veterans it is the bedrock of the term "survivor's guilt." Both groups remember those they were forced or chose to leave behind: those who were killed or maimed even as they escaped. For refugees there is the added humiliation of having been unable to provide food, shelter, and clothing for themselves and their families, of being portrayed by indifferent media outlets as needy children or self-seeking indigents. Both refugees and veterans are left to wonder at a fate that would let some prosper and others fail, stunned by their good fortune, the result of luck or acts of self-preservation that, in certain lights, to some might appear only selfish. For veterans, such conflicted feelings may be further complicated by the ways our nation reported the war, imagining its soldiers alternately as stone-faced killers of Third World innocents, or traumatized heroes on a politically hapless mission. Thinking about my uncle and his silence about the war, I realize that some part of him may have worried that his combat experience would be seen as either a psychological liability or an admission of moral guilt: to tell us about having fought in Vietnam could be tantamount to admitting he'd taken part in the My Lai massacre.

And the shame of having experienced war, Trinh shows me now, might have particularly harsh consequences for men, even down the generations. Though boys in Vietnam are prized, maleness might be a curse when it comes to war, where the bulk of fighting falls on male shoulders. In America, combat experience is no longer a requirement for masculinity, but the myths surrounding manhood are still attached to martial values: aggression, discipline, an almost pathological drive to acquire power. In nations historically and imaginatively defined by war—nations that include both Vietnam and America—young men might be more likely to measure themselves against violence's yardstick. This may in part explain what Trinh also notes about her community: the continued attraction of young Vietnamese men to gang life. I myself wonder, briefly, if Ly's attack on white men was not an act of self-hatred only, but a more complex bid to be seen, by both Americans and Vietnamese, as a man.

For understanding your identity is not, as Trinh's childhood friendships suggest, as simple as looking to other groups to choose your race and gender roles. Just because you aren't white, you don't suddenly become Chicano or black. Just because you fought in a war, your combat experience doesn't make you equal to the men you fought alongside, or even a man. In the post-1975 rush to house the growing tide of refugees, Vietnamese received preferential treatment in the assignment of low-income housing, often at the expense of black and Chicano families. In Grier Heights, North Carolina, African Americans complained that the Vietnamese received support even though they "did not die in World War I and World War II as [their own] fathers and grandfathers" did. In both black and Chicano communities, refugees were seen not as fellow combatants but opportunistic welfare seekers. If their military service was considered, it was to hold refugees responsible for the loss of American family members during war, and this, along with the fact that Southeast Asians suddenly absorbed the bulk of already scarce social services, led to scapegoating and outbreaks of violence.

Vietnamese military service and Vietnamese suffering in support of America did not make wartime experiences, or loyalties, equivalent. To some Americans, Vietnamese ex-soldiers were not portrayed or seen as men, but infantilized dependents. When it came time to relocate refugees on our shores, war thus became the crucible not of American citizenship but American responsibility, all other contributions by the South Vietnamese military conveniently erased.

There are many such ways that Southeast Asian men have been erased in America. For example, currently the most common symbol of Vietnamese success is the nail salon: a multibillion-dollar industry that's largely woman-owned and woman-operated. Southeast Asian women are portrayed both as ideal entrepreneurs and ideal blue-collar workers, the backbone of sweatshops and the beauty industry, as well as budding tiger moms. Added to this is the fantasy of the Asian woman as hyperfeminized or hypersexualized, the only upside to this stereotype being that it gives Asian women a presence in the media that Asian men lack. Southeast Asian men, like other Asian men in America, have to contend with notions of masculinity assembled in the late nineteenth century, when U.S. immigration policies allowed

Chinese men to immigrate to the United States but kept women out for fear that they would breed. Social stigmas limited work to railroads, sugar cane production, and washing other people's laundry, the result being that Asian men were characterized in newspapers as either sex-starved brutes or, alternately, effete members of "bachelor societies" whose laundry work, braided hair, and long robes resembled the labor and clothing of Western women.

Asian male success in America has long been cast around the experiences of Chinese, Korean, and Japanese male immigrants who came to the States with more education and resources, and often more by choice than by the need to flee a traumatizing crisis. Stateside, they slowly grew supportive communities over time, which offered them economic connections and local health centers able to cater to their needs, as well as any necessary physical security that might kick in where the state's legal protection would not. Southeast Asian refugees had few of these assets. In contrast to other East Asians, Southeast Asians were forcibly relocated to communities utterly unlike their own, where fathers and uncles may have been absent—whether due to being killed in war, or because they had been sent to different American towns than their families—or where male authority figures suffered from PTSD. All of these things meant that a young Vietnamese American man's place in his new country could be, as Trinh suggests, vulnerable, and his self-perception "mostly negative." Social anxiety, isolation, and passivity such as her brother's may be the flip side of wartime violence, or at least the other end of its continuum. Though I can find no studies that prove this, I wonder whether Southeast Asian men are implicitly at a greater risk than Southeast Asian women for being socially anxious and depressed, something that neither Vietnamese nor Americans, both belonging to patriarchal cultures, can see, because we do not want to see it. Thinking this, I am reminded suddenly of a story one young man told during an interview about his relocation to the States. For months after school, he said, because his parents worked in the evenings and because he had no friends to meet, he would go to the local mall and wander there alone, looking in shop windows, sitting in the courtyard, watching this new world of strangers moving together, talking, eating. He never bought anything, he said. What could he buy that would make him as happy as these people seemed, strangers that he spied upon and studied, trying to memorize how they dressed and turned their heads and smiled, how they took each other's hands so casually? Perhaps that was why he went, he told me, sounding almost angry. To watch how these strangers could touch each other so easily.

My father, when I was in high school, told me that some of his happiest days were spent in the Air Force. An only child for most of his childhood, he'd been raised on a suburban farm by his mother and grandmother, far from other families with children. He contracted polio the summer he turned eight and spent the next several months of his life in a hospital, cut off from his cousins and family. In high school, with his hips and back still weakened by the disease, he'd stayed away from both girls and sports, ashamed of his thinness and uneasiness with exercise. The military, as unlikely an institution I could ever imagine my father choosing to join, provided him with a kind of companionship he'd never had as a child: it gave him physical training and strength, and must have made him feel, for the first time, truly an equal with the other men around him.

I wonder if my uncle's silence was not just shame or reticence, a way of shielding his mother from the terrifying details of combat, but a more complex loyalty he wanted to show his fellow soldiers: an understanding that he, like they, would keep secret the violence they each had suffered and together enacted, a silent and proud oath of fellowship to men whom he may also have recognized did not always include him in that fellowship. My uncle is not the image of the soldier my teachers described at school when we studied Tim O'Brien's *The Things They Carried*, nor what the news showed when reporters talked about veterans; it was not men like my uncle who served in the wars as popularly portrayed in movies. In fact, it was men who looked like my uncle who'd caused the deaths of Americans in Korea, the Philippines, and Vietnam. As the black protests against Vietnamese immigrants in North Carolina proved, a shared experience of war does not necessarily bring combatants and victims together. It does not cohere men or communities, even if they are historically on the same side. As Komunyakaa's poem shows, civic identity is ultimately a choice, hard-won and self-negating, requiring that at some level people overlook their own histories.

During the Vietnamese refugee crisis, America congratulated itself on the numbers of people it passed through its processing centers, treating the body count as evidence of its commitment, the greatest measure of our moral and political responsibility. In measuring the refugees this way, the United States treated refugees as a stream of individuals rather than interconnected communities, demanding their reinvention as U.S. citizens by acting as if the past mattered less than the present, as if identity and culture were endlessly adaptable. With the refugees, we did something essentially American: we divorced the idea of citizenship from race and ethnicity, something that, within and without the United States, many struggle to imagine, because we do not simply fashion our identities, we also inherit them. Similarly, upon their repatriation, we asked our veterans to divorce their combat memories from their ideas of home. We asked them, implicitly, not to tell us what they'd done and seen. In turn, when it came to protecting the men who suffered with and from that violence, we acted out of love and stayed silent. Trinh's reticence to speak about her brother parallels my uncle's silence, and the steadfastness the black soldier displays in Komunyakaa's poem. Each is an act of loyalty that comes at the cost of willful forgetting: it is a kind of delusion based not on history, but hope.

A kind of hope that Trinh still recalls about her own childhood in America: how her early years in Poteet felt like one endless period of waiting for something to happen, for something inflexible in her life to change. For many years, childhood was not, strangely, all that different from the camp life she and her brother experienced as refugees. Recalling it now, she describes a day her brother fell ill: first a fever, then a series of violent, jolting seizures that shook and then paralyzed his young body, sending her mother screaming for help. Trinh remembers her father standing to one side, silently watching his wife command their daughter to find somebody: a doctor, a nurse, anyone who could help them. Trinh, panicked, began to run through the camp's makeshift warren of cabins, their gray lines of tarps and drying laundry. But no one stepped forward to help. Perhaps it was because they were unsure of what she wanted, or perhaps it was because each one assumed another among these hundreds of strangers would be better qualified. Regardless, she and her brother were on their own. That's what Trinh thinks about when she thinks of that day: an eight-year-old girl, spattered with mud, unable to get help for her brother.

6 Trauma, once it takes root in the body, is difficult to heal. According to the National Vietnam Veterans Longitudinal Study, even forty years after the war, roughly 11 percent of veterans still suffer from flashbacks, PTSD, depression, and other mental health disorders. This is ten times the rate of veterans who did not serve in Vietnam. The effects of these veterans' health problems on their communities can increase exponentially. Judith Broder, a psychiatrist who works with The Soldiers Project in California, says that one troubled veteran affects at least ten relatives and friends: she compares the effects of a traumatized veteran in his community to someone throwing a pebble in water. The ripples "keep expanding and expanding," as Broder said in a recent National Public Radio interview. "It's horrifying, actually."

If trauma is hard to heal in individuals, it is even harder to heal in families. Because of the number of wars and attempts at genocide in the twentieth century, we know there is a strong association between parents' traumatic symptoms and those of their children. In study after study, researchers find that parents who have experienced war, genocide, internment, or colonization have children that display increased rates of antisocial behaviors. Studies of the descendants of the Holocaust, the Armenian genocide, the Japanese American internment camps, the Khmer Rouge genocide, and other victims of trauma suggest that the effects of communal trauma get passed down through the generations. While individual communities, and individuals within these communities, express these inherited traumas differently, stress, anxiety, depression, food hoarding, and drug or alcohol abuse mark the descendants of survivors, even down to the third generation. These behaviorally inherited traumas can be found across cultures and nationalities, and can be found in the families of war veterans and refugees alike.

Linked to this research are the number of epigenetic studies that suggest trauma has biological effects on individuals, effects that aren't just behaviorally transmitted, but are physically transmitted also. A widely read 2014 *Nature Neuroscience* article discusses a study done with mice that suggests early-life exposure to traumatic events alters micro-RNA expression, as well as behavioral and metabolic responses in the offspring of traumatized mice. Injecting sperm RNA from traumatized mice into fertilized eggs of nontraumatized mice reproduces the behavior and metabolic changes of the traumatized mouse in its progeny. Social experiences physically change the body, hard-wiring the genes to make both the sufferer and his or her children susceptible to PTSD, anxiety, and depression, a vulnerability reflected in our very neurons and cells.

Trauma may have another, darker genetic inheritance as well. Neuropsychologists have identified other heritable traits that appear to push people towards risky situations and behaviors: attention deficit disorder, difficulty processing one's memory, a lack of self-control. For example, recent studies have shown that significantly more American Indians experience at least one traumatic incident—whether rape or assault, car accident or crime—than other Americans, while at the same time their risk of being assaulted or inheriting PTSD is heritable to a similar degree. Essentially, a person who inherits trauma may, due to biology and a host of historical forces outside of her control, seek out or fall victim to other traumatizing events.

Whether the cause of transgenerational trauma is genetic, behavioral, or a combination of both, trauma is not only a medical condition. Trauma is both a physical and a figurative legacy, moving between bodily symptoms and the self's symbolic reimaginings, changing even our concept of time. As Freud argued, trauma is not just an isolated past event but a recurrence, what trauma theorist Cathy Caruth calls a "continuous retelling" of grief. For the traumatized individual and her child, war and relocation thus must be repeatedly confronted, not only as a means of minimizing their terrors, but as a way of acknowledging the astonishing fact of survival. We might call this one of the effects of what the critic Marianne Hirsch labels "postmemory": "the experience of being separated in time and space from the war being remembered, yet of living with the eyewitness memory." In a sense, the memory that a parent unspools in her retelling of the past is transferred to her child, reimagined or reconstituted in her own mind's eye.

In the refugee community, war marks time. It cleaves it, as it divides a family's life into events that happened "before the war" or "after the war." In some families, it splits personalities: the father the child had before war and relocation, and the father she had after. Trauma is a broken country—one in which the past fractures into the present, stuck like glass shards into skin, or sutured together like a tape reel from a thousand fragmented recordings. To live in this country is to traverse borders between self and other that are inherently subjective and constantly shifting, where violence erupts without warning, and where grief, silence, guilt, and shame come to feel as natural, and as necessary, as breathing. It is a place with no beginning or ending, where memories become intertwined. And if you are a child, it is a region where any boundary between yourself and your parent is not only unstable, but may ultimately be indefensible.

"Sociopathic" is how Diana Khoi Nguyen describes her mother, the middle child of a large and prosperous family of pharmacists from Saigon. Diana's grandfather worked at the U.S. embassy as a translator. He was an authoritative man so famously stubborn that none of his family dared question his belief that the South would win the war. His refusal to flee meant that only at the very last second did the family choose to act. They chose by allowing Diana's grandfather to gather up all the sons in the family and run with them to meet the airlift out of Saigon. The girls and women, including Diana's mother and her grandmother, who worked as a pharmacist, remained: stunned, frightened, and alone.

Diana's mother's memories from that day forward are of shame and terror: shame for being left, and terror of a world in which dead bodies could be found in the streets, her friends and neighbors vanished now, hiding at home. Once, out for bread, her mother stumbled into the path of a North Vietnamese tank careening down the road, driven so haphazardly it seemed as if the machine were helmed by a child, the tank plowing up and over sidewalks at random, crushing café chairs and tables. At school, she found that suddenly books she'd read had been rewritten for a changed regime; in the city, the street signs were repainted with the names of communist leaders. Overnight, French and English became forbidden languages. Diana's mother, over the summer, was sent to a re-education camp to learn, among other skills, how to shoot. She shook when the instructor handed her the rifle, crying that it felt too heavy to shoot.

It was a childhood that tilted between panic and uncertainty, and once Diana's mother arrived in the United States—smuggled out to Malaysia on a fishing boat whose captain family friends had bribed with gold—she forced herself to repress these memories. She became an engineer, then met and married Diana's father, a man who had also escaped Saigon. They had three children together: Diana; Diana's younger brother, Oliver; and a sister, Denise. They bought a house in Rancho Palos Verdes, an affluent, white Los Angeles neighborhood as far away from any of the other Asian groups her mother disliked as they could get. The war receded into the past, erupting again only at moments of stress in which Diana's mother returned home from work in a rage, slapping her children, screaming. There were curses, threats, there were sudden physical attacks so frightening they drove Diana's father from the house, while trapping the children inside it. One night, Diana's mother sat her children down at the kitchen table and asked, "Do you remember the story of the woman who sewed her children into their car seats so they couldn't escape, then drove them off a bridge to drown? I'm going to do that to all of you tonight. Because none of you deserves to live."

By the time she reached adolescence, Diana would learn to protect herself from her mother by never showing any kind of pleasure or distress that her mother could use against her later. As an adult, she'd struggle with depression and guilt; she'd learn to classify herself as a "high-functioning" depressive only after her time at Columbia, where student medical insurance allowed her to get therapy. But her siblings got worse. Diana's sister, now in her twenties, once so shy she would urinate in class rather than ask a teacher excuse her, still lives at home, unable to work. Diana's younger brother, Oliver, suffers from fits so violent that Diana's mother, uncharacteristically, has begun to beg Diana to make him see a psychiatrist. These days, Oliver has stopped speaking altogether. For the past two years, he's lived as a shadow in his parents' back bedroom, vibrating with a silent rage. Besides sneaking into the kitchen for food when the family sleeps, his only excursions out of his room are to slip all the family photos from their frames, in order to slice out his family members' faces.

What do we think we mean when we say we say that trauma is inherited? Beyond the science, does it mean that familial grief is like an object or ideal, something that exists outside of us as much as it may reside inside us, and therefore something we can ultimately divorce ourselves from, jettisoning it from our lives like an unfortunate title, or a house that no one wants? Or does it mean exactly what the science suggests: that it is indelibly part of us, scars not just on the body but on the soul? Does this mean there is never any getting rid of grief? Does it mean that we are cursed?

It is tempting to chalk Oliver's anger up solely to war's dark inheritance, just as it may be tempting to attribute the years of physical and emotional abuse that Diana, her siblings, and her father suffered to her mother's wartime experience, but Diana resists this reading. Largely, she says, she resists this idea because of the mental resilience displayed by her aunts and uncles, who also lived through the war. In Diana's family, her mother is the outlier, and whether out of shame or loyalty, none of her other family members stepped in to protect her children. Filial piety and discipline are jealously upheld social values in Southeast Asian culture, and both have allowed Diana's mother to give free rein to her attacks. Because of this complex intersection of nature, nurture, and history, and because, I suspect, Diana wants also to believe she is not at her body's mercy, that she can abandon this lacerating inheritance science suggests that she's been given, it is hard for her to differentiate what is war-induced trauma, and what might be her mother's innate mental disorder. What, essentially, is just bad luck.

There may be a danger, I suspect, in relying too heavily on the science regarding trauma. It potentially satisfies our desires to see certain people as beyond our help and responsibility. It makes us passive in the face of great suffering, including our own. But perhaps it also allows us to forgive each other. If Diana can never determine what caused her mother's disorder, she can see that her mother's mental illness stunted her siblings and herself: in that sense, they are direct products of their mother's rages, which the war may have triggered, a war that might, in Diana's most forgiving moments, both contextualize and even soften, slightly, the blows of her mother's anger.

Beta-blockers, drugs that fix the aftershocks of PTSD by blocking the amygdala's consolidation of fearful memories, and counseling for pregnant mothers suffering PTSD: all of these have been proposed to counteract the genetic effects of trauma. Science is trying to provide us an end point: a place where pain finally resides and, because it can be located, can be healed. But the complex ways that body and culture intertwine suggest that some part of this effort to locate pain may be a fantasy. You heal the physical symptoms of PTSD, but you don't change war's impact on generations of culture, an impact that resonates not through physical bodies, but through language and memory, art and song. And even if you could mitigate war's impacts, for some, these interventions may be a little late. More than forty years after the fall of the Khmer Rouge, for example, the children of Cambodian survivors still have not economically advanced in ways that children of other Asian immigrants and refugees have. Nearly half of all Cambodians in America lack a high school diploma, and only a little more than 10 percent have a college degree. Trauma and PTSD have riven Cambodian communities across the country, with one counseling service in Massachusetts estimating that 95 percent of the Cambodians they treat have been diagnosed with PTSD.

When considering why so many Southeast Asians struggle in America, we recite the practicalities of their pasts: so many arrived with little education and no English, without money, leaving countries out of desperation rather than choice. Now we're asked to see these practicalities as extending to their bodies, the genes they carry inside them, expressed or controlled through a complicated mix of heritability and luck. Nationally, Vietnamese Americans have the highest rate of incarceration among Asians, and gang culture offers a popular alternative for young Vietnamese, Hmong, and Laotian men who can't find jobs. Perhaps these are not only economic but genetic inheritances, we argue, ones we could have mitigated with therapeutic attention—as we might have softened the shock of arrival with long-term English language classes, with work-training programs that did not slot refugees into only blue-collar jobs.

This may be another reason why the epigenetic research discomfits me: regardless of its scientific truth, depending on how we use these facts about the physical markers of trauma on the body, we may dangerously approach replicating the arguments used against Asian immigrants in the past, such as the ones we use to deny entrance to Syrian refugees now. Refugees are a contagion, some argue. They hide within their midst potential spies or subversives, their bodies packed with illness. Unruled and potentially unruly, they live outside the modern laws we depend upon, and now also outside of the genetic profiles that would make them easily governable. In this, the refugee becomes a symbol, not just of the stateless individual seeking a home, but of the unending traumas of war, which make them potentially criminal.

To treat the historical wound through a genetic fact seems, at some point, also to dodge another kind of responsibility. To heal the physical wound might allow certain institutions to claim that they've redressed past wrongs in which they've also played a significant part. There is more than one source for trauma and PTSD in the refugee communities that have fled to the United States, and this list includes our modern politics.

In "We Refugees," Hannah Arendt writes that the refugee reminds us of the limits of human rights, not just for the refugee, but for us all. Those relocated to new nations from concentration camps, she writes, "in order to forget more efficiently" the past, refuse to allude to the horrors they left, understanding that "nobody wants to know that contemporary history has created a new kind of human beings—the kind that are put in concentration camps by their foes and in internment camps by their friends." The refugee is not only a fugitive, but a reminder that our states, when acting upon and against each other in war, constrain some part of all our futures.

"We think of our bodies as stable biological structures that live in the world but are fundamentally separate from it," UCLA genetic researcher Steve Cole says about his work in epigenetics. "But what we're learning from the molecular processes that actually keep our bodies running is that we're far more fluid than we realize, and the world passes through us." According to this logic, epigenetic research reminds us not of the heritable flaws we may be individually or communally punished for, but of the collective duty we have to each other. Our politics and histories intimately link us. If the modern state is the source of law and technology, innovation and order, it is also the source of the horrors that can and have rewired the minds and bodies of our children. In that sense, our global politics are also our domestic health policies.

On Christmas Eve, I wake to an email sent from Diana, who reports that she is on her way to a family funeral. A week earlier, her brother, Oliver, committed suicide. "I thought of you once I landed in California and felt an update pertinent to your current research," she writes. "I know that he doesn't directly pertain to the case of the young Vietnamese man in SLC, but this is certainly another sad outcome of mental illness in first-generation Vietnamese-Americans."

Her brother was twenty-four years old.

7 On April 4, 1991, four young Vietnamese men drove into the parking lot of a Sacramento Good Guys Electronics store with two nine-millimeter pistols and a handgun. It would be their second hastily planned robbery of the day. Weeks before, the men had sworn allegiance to a loosely affiliated gang called "The Oriental Boys," and, perhaps as proof of their seriousness, perhaps for show, they'd bragged that they would hold up a local store. Their first robbery they unhappily botched, so the Good Guys robbery would be their last-ditch attempt to make good on their promise. Cuong Tran, seventeen, and three brothers, Long Khac Nguyen, seventeen, Pham Khac Nguyen, nineteen, and Loi Khac Nguyen, twenty-one, burst in to the electronics store screaming at customers and staff to get down on their knees, then herded the panicked shoppers into the back of the store near a bank of windows. Over the course of eight and a half hours, they would hold forty-one people hostage, killing three and wounding more than eleven, shooting them at close range before dozens of television screens flickering on the store's display shelves.

For many hours, it was unclear what the young men wanted. The sheriff at the scene that day said they "were attempting to gain notoriety" in their gang, while hostages later suggested they wanted to be movie stars. In an interview with a *Chicago Tribune* reporter published later, one of the surviving hostages, Charles Rangel, who had been shot point-blank in the right ankle and left knee, said that they "just wanted to go back [to Vietnam]."

The young men themselves spent the day alternately demanding bullet-proof vests, four million dollars in cash, dozens of thousand-year-old ginseng roots, and a helicopter to fly them to Thailand. Finally, after a few hours, they were they able to come to a consensus. They wanted to draw media attention to the plight of Vietnam, they announced via a bleeding hostage. They wanted to kill Viet Cong; they themselves were on a suicide mission. In fact, it did turn out to be a suicide mission: during the crisis, three of the young men were shot and killed by police after the police set off concussion grenades, shattering the store's tall bank of windows. Only Loi Khac Nguyen, the eldest of the group, survived. He was subsequently tried and sentenced to forty-one consecutive life terms in prison. To date, the hostage rescue operation is the largest in U.S. history.

The three young men were post-1975 refugees. According to a 1991 *Los Angeles Times* article, the Nguyens came to the States after escaping Vietnam aboard a fishing boat on which they'd spent seven months at sea and at anchor off the coast of Malaysia, routinely raided by pirates. Sons of a low-ranking South Vietnamese soldier, the Nguyen boys spent four months in an Indonesian refugee camp before arriving with their parents in California in 1980, penniless, terrified, and unable to speak English. According to the article, though the Nguyen brothers attended American public schools and began slowly to adjust to their new culture, the Nguyen parents struggled, never learning enough English to find steady work. During the hostage crisis, the Nguyens' mother apparently rushed to the store to persuade her sons to give themselves up, but the sheriff refused to let her speak with them; likely, he did not fully understand her request.

A 2000 play, *The Good Guys: An American Tragedy*, by Michael Edo Keane and Miko Lee, imagines the boys' backstory prior to this hostage-taking, including a relationship with a domineering ex-soldier father whose expectations they cannot meet, and their longing for a homeland to which they can never return. *The Good Guys* highlights what might be the crime's most striking similarity to Ly's case: the violent attempt of young Vietnamese American men to reframe their own version of the war. Reading over past articles on the crisis, I am struck by a sentence in a 1991 *New York Times* article that locates the event within a swelling crime-ridden Asian population around Sacramento. According to the article, the Nguyens' hostage-taking is just one more example of the ways that refugees fall "easy prey" to Vietnamese gangs who "specialize in home invasions, in which family members are tortured until they reveal the hiding places of gold or jewelry." The reporter suggests these young men's actions are, to an extent, typical in a culture of chronic gang violence, and this, along with the fact that the *Times* ignores the Nguyens' last stated desire to fight the Viet Cong, does not take seriously any possibility that the men were acting out in response to the legacy of war.

The Nguyens' relatives and neighbors also seemed reluctant to make this connection, preferring instead to blame laissez-faire American attitudes toward child rearing. If non-Vietnamese Americans saw the crime as reflecting a problem within Vietnamese culture, Vietnamese Americans saw the crime as reflecting a problem within mainstream American culture. One of the Nguyens' acquaintances blamed assimilating to Western values for the hostage crisis, saying, "In America, there is too much freedom. We cannot tell the kids what to do. They were nice guys but they grew up in this country. They watched TV. They learned a lot of bad things."

The Nguyen brothers appear in the papers as both too American and not American enough, but what strikes me most about the portrayal of their crime is how the Nguyens, during the moment of their crime, turned their birth nation into a fantasy unlike any real Vietnam. Exactly how, in 1991, were they to distinguish the Viet Cong from any other Vietnamese citizens? The Nguyens' final request of the police was to mourn an ideal: to turn their crime into a memorial for a country that no longer existed. In the Nguyens' memorial, Vietnam is a real country to which they cannot return, but it is also a figurative one from which they have never departed.

The symbol of Vietnam that the Nguyens created is one of perpetual brokenness, a pain that cannot end.

In that, the Nguyens' is a very American imagining of Vietnam. Had they remained in the country of their birth, they would have seen and experienced its changes; because they were separated from it, it became a fictive nation outside of time. It is one of the reasons my friends in Vietnam are so adamantly disinterested in talking about the war: if the country can't evolve in the outsider's imagination, neither can its people. The Nguyens, having spent so many years in the States, by this time had become almost more American than Vietnamese, strangers now to the culture of their birth country. The Vietnamese are often portrayed in our movies and books about the Vietnam War as relics of the past, their values and institutional systems framed as rejections of modernity. To me, the Nguyens' imagination of Vietnam seems as likely assembled from images that the American media provided them as from those provided by their families. Theirs is similar to Ly's fantasy of Vietnam, his chanted cry in the Smith's parking lot, "Why did you kill my people?" suggesting the erasure of his South Vietnamese past to recast himself as a Northern Vietnamese victim. To me, it is an explicitly American reimagining of himself, one in which he is both enemy and victim, the perpetual alien the United States cannot subjugate.

As I spend months researching trauma and memory, it strikes me that there's another term, cultural trauma, to describe what the Nguyen brothers experienced. Cultural trauma is a theory that suggests trauma is contagious, that the narrating of historical events might begin to unite the experiences of actual survivors with those who never directly witnessed war. The theory of transgenerational trauma, which argues that children can genetically inherit their parents' PTSD, runs alongside cultural trauma, but is different in that transgenerational trauma runs along a more restricted, familial course. Cultural trauma, on the other hand, radiates far out past family boundaries, transmitted to others not through genetics but through the representation of traumatic events, whether in person, in families, or through the media. In that sense, trauma is not an individual wound, but an infection.

On the Internet, trying to find the connection between storytelling and trauma, I come across a website devoted to helping PTSD sufferers create what it calls "trauma narratives" for healing. "Telling the trauma story is one of the most effective coping strategies for dealing with trauma-related distress," reads the PTSD Trauma Treatment website. "Talking about a traumatic experience helps organize memories and feelings into a more manageable and understandable psychological 'package.'" I am interested in this idea of trauma as a "package," something material, even transferrable: a box one could pick up and lock away in the corner of a closet shelf, perhaps. The idea that trauma can be treated through narrative is appealing, since narrative depends upon the organization of time, while by its very nature trauma disorders time. Implicit in the website's mission, however, is the idea that time can also be forcibly reordered to bring one's traumatic history in line with an audience's desire for a more artful story: for whom, exactly, is the trauma narrative being "managed"? In that sense, narrative therapy might address the root of the PTSD problem by encouraging patients to learn how they can reconstruct their own memories, not through the guileless recitation of past traumas but through carefully plotted stories that privilege an audience's catharsis and revelation over private suffering.

"There was no narrative," Mai-Linh Hong, a young PhD student, tells me about her life. "Even when I was six or seven years old, I heard horrible stories about people who had fled but hadn't survived. Stories of people adrift on boats, of cannibalism, of people who drowned at sea. It was terrifying. I couldn't sleep." Mai-Linh is speaking to me over Skype from her apartment in New York. Like Diana, she's a writer, and perhaps for this reason she returns, repeatedly, to the incomplete nature of her parents' stories. None of them had a beginning or end, she tells me now, which meant that images of the past drifted in through the open door of her bedroom at night, or through the kitchen at family parties: shards of other people's nightmares pieced together but unorganized. It was these stories' very fragmentary nature that made them so frightening, their refusal to cohere into stories, into closed structures, as if their horror could erupt at any point into her daily life.

Listening to her, I am reminded of my own experience reading Charles Reznikoff's *Holocaust*, a book of poems constructed of verbatim quotations from the Eichmann trial testimony of Holocaust survivors. Reznikoff's poems collage together survivors' spare, unsentimental testimony about camp life, torture, genocide. Characters appear in one stanza only to disappear in the next, images of grotesque violence flame up and are as quickly extinguished. The poems lurch across time, moving backward and forward, but with no one protagonist to carry the reader through. Though conversational in tone, the poems are not conversations: they are assemblages of voices, choruses of half-finished terror.

The poems are meant to resist a reader's identification with their speakers: because I cannot follow any individual or story to conclusion, my sense of catharsis is diminished, even rejected; I am numbed, not moved. Reznikoff, an American-born Jew, admitted to the literary scholar Milton Hindus that he resisted writing any poems at all about the Holocaust for thirty years after the genocide, a hesitation Hindus attributed to the problems of trauma testimony itself as a genre. About this, Hindus wrote:

> If even the expressions of survivors sometimes seemed to be little better than exploitative "Kitsch" and those of others more sincere and genuine proved repetitive, diminishing and sentimental, was it possible for an American Jew to do any better? There was an abyss of cliché, propaganda and editorialism in the subject which even the wariest writer might have difficulty in avoiding. Was it possible, then, that the central event of Jewish history in almost two

thousand years defied the imagination and had best be surrounded by silence?

The idea that the testimony of a genocide survivor could ever seem to be "kitsch" might be anathema to the contemporary reader. But as a writer, I understand that narrating anything, even trauma, relies upon using literary conventions: character and plot, heroes and villains, symbols, metaphor. We rely on stock images to engage the emotions of our listeners, understanding that these clichés may be more easily imaginable, even thrilling, than more inventive choices. Conventions can bring speaker and listener into closer emotional proximity, but they also risk making those who have not suffered trauma feel as if, having heard the testimony, they too might have suffered. In doing this, these conventions risk diminishing the experience of victims over time by raising the spectator's emotions to the imagined level of another victim. But Reznikoff believed that the testimony of the Jewish genocide was primarily for Jews. The Holocaust included many groups and people, but it was not a genocide of *all* groups and people. Reznikoff's fragmentary poems resist the gentile reader's desire to empathize with any particular speaker or subject, effectively blocking her from imagining that she has in any way "experienced" the Holocaust. For Reznikoff, the goal was not to assimilate trauma into memory; it was perhaps more mimetic: to make that horror forever inconceivable, unadaptable, the specific and horrific legacy of being Jewish.

Over months of listening to people's traumatic stories, I have learned how enervated and nervous each conversation makes me. It takes hours to come down from an interview, because the stories are intense to process, but also because of how easily I slip into them, imagining and elaborating on the details myself, which might also keep me from accurately hearing them. Sometimes, sitting in my car alone after a particularly emotional interview, I find myself shaking. What I hear both invites and repels me as a listener, and if at times I am not sure whether I am the one who should be listening, I am also not sure in what ways my presence, my own nationality and race, has helped shape, for the worse, the stories being told.

But listening to other people's stories also makes me feel, increasingly, responsible for retelling them: over the hours I spend with each person, I begin to feel a gnawing sense of doom. It is not that I feel traumatized by the details of my interviewees' lives; instead, I worry how I will fail them if I cannot relate these stories to a larger audience. And so, as I transcribe my interviews for an imagined reader, I, too, find myself slipping into conventions of storytelling to make these stories more vivid for a reader. I tell myself that this is the value of literature: to help a reader see and feel an image, to make that image come alive in her body, which itself is the starting point for empathy. And yet it is also a way to distract me from what, at root, is inexpressible: at best, narrative is only a translation of suffering, and all translations are limited, partial renditions of their originals that also, inevitably, transform their originals. To narrativize a trauma like war, or domestic violence, or a stabbing, which feels enormous, would be to turn it into something shaped and static: a slab of stone, a poem, a wrapped package. This is the paradox of writing about or even recounting trauma: the conventions you use to express experience may make these same experiences less actually palpable. Better, perhaps, as Hindus noted, to descend into silence. I return to wondering, what did that young man walking the perimeter of Ground Zero want as he repeated his tale of terror and survival? To invite tourists to share his pain as a way of better understanding the site? Or to use us as a screen onto which he could forever project his traumatic fantasies? Did the repetition of that day ever heal his pain, I wonder, or did it just train him to be a better storyteller?

8 According to the testimony of several hostages taken during the Good Guys hostage crisis, the Nguyen brothers briefly expressed a desire to be film stars. Interestingly, it was film that introduced an American audience to many of the combat horrors that are now de rigueur in war-based literature and cinema. If the Vietnam War gave us the term PTSD, the now more than four hundred films about Vietnam also gave us the primary ways we visualize it. Even *flashback* is a term taken from film, and researchers who examined war records from the Victorian era up to Vietnam found that references to soldiers experiencing flashbacks were practically nonexistent before the age of film. And since war films are the way in which most of us come to be familiar with war, they may shape the way that veterans upon return frame and heal from their own combat experiences.

Narrative, as a way of both anticipating and healing from trauma, suggests an ordered chronology where, in reality, there rarely is one. Narrative shapes communities through shared language and imagery, but it also divides these same communities when facts no longer cohere with collective memory. In a sense, a successful trauma narrative recalls the effects of cultural assimilation: it asks its narrators to suppress the power of their individual experiences in service to the communal story. For those with a gift for storytelling, narrative may allow for the explication of a parent's traumatized silence, allowing a child to invent or organize details that might explain a father's implacable authoritarianism, a mother's rages. The parent's history may remain his own, but the guilt and shame and terror that defined his past: these a family learns to share. The child reaches for images, a framework. She reaches for anything, true or false, that the surrounding culture will give her.

And yet few of us want to imagine that a violent history might rely on anything false: it is authenticity, not fabrication, that earns the traumatized victim our sympathy. So, for instance, when confronted with migrants who commit violence in the name of war without themselves having been war's original victims, we might choose to dismiss their trauma or to explain it away with neurological science. Both reactions reveal how deeply we privilege and even fetishize "real" claims to pain. Even as I gather articles for my research, I suspect my fascination with epigenetics is a way to justify Ly's crime by pointing to evidence that will authenticate what I would otherwise never take seriously. But as a writer, I also know that if something reads as true, we tend to treat it as true. And part of a narrative's being judged as "true" relies on its being entertaining: in that sense, audience enjoyment matters. Narrativizing trauma is about proving that one's victimization occurred by garnering an audience's sympathy: itself an act of organizing the elements of one's trauma in the most entertaining, and perhaps deliberate, way.

If trauma is both an event and a genetic injury, a wound carved into the body as well as into the mind, then it is both a fact and a story. Ly and the Nguyens may not have personally experienced war, and they may have distorted the war's historic details, but they have not missed its deep impact on their families' lives. Ly and the Nguyens are both right and wrong, figurative and literal, when they cite the Vietnam War as any kind of "reason" for their attacks. Metaphors, when they work, highlight otherwise unseen connections between events: they make us see something true, through the lens of something deliberately constructed, artful, false.

Vietnam is a metaphor for nonrefugee Americans, as much as it is a country. "Let's not make this another Vietnam" was the recurring phrase I heard throughout my college years about the first Gulf War, a phrase that has since been repeated throughout our more recent wars in Iraq and Afghanistan. When we speak about the trauma of the Vietnam War, audience determines whose trauma we refer to: American veterans or Vietnamese ones, soldiers or citizens, men or women. The war itself has become an all-encompassing image trotted out to suggest everything from napalmed children, to raped women, to returned amputees spat upon in American malls. I don't mean to be glib in this recitation of horrors, but to point out how formulaic, perhaps even "kitsch" they have become. *Vietnam* has been aestheticized for us through a host of movies and television shows, through novels and poems, which, though shot through with the real pain of actual survivors, still rely upon certain conventions to be told. *Vietnam* is a rhetorical device employed by senators running for office, and as such *Vietnam* relies upon distilling war's terror to a single word that we use as political currency.

But of course, in Vietnam, the war they fought with us is called "The American War," and so we have become a metaphor in turn: a symbol of brute militarism, of colonial and Cold War anxieties. Perhaps that is the metaphor Ly also reached for during his attack, his *America*—like his *Vietnam*—a country of aggression and displacement, as much as it is a space of mental illness and addiction. His *America*, like his *Vietnam*, is another country outside of time, locked in a loop of unending conflict. That is perhaps the most ingenious feature of his crime: as a metaphor, the crime suggests how deeply he's attached himself to a grievance without end. The metaphor of war makes him both visible and invisible, the one lost as well as the one losing. In his narrative, there is no possible redress to the wound of his deracination.

I wonder how much my interviewees and I use *America* or *Vietnam* as such metaphorical currency between us, how much we rely on these words to fill in the narrative blanks when the pain of actual facts threatens to fill up the room. Perhaps I have been drawn to cases like Ly's and the Nguyens' because Vietnam has been such a powerful symbol for my family, too. My father enlisted in the Air Force believing both that it would fast-track him into the Monterey language school, but also believing that it was his duty as an American to serve his country. His decision was part patriotism, part calculation: a plan that almost backfired when the Air Force background check uncovered that, as a young teen, my father had briefly subscribed to a Wobbly newsletter. Still, while his college and graduate school colleagues finished up their degrees and found jobs, my father served as a weatherman for the Air Force in Turkey, and when his time finished four years later, he returned to find that the academic job market was now fully stocked with men who hadn't served. He referred often to Vietnam during my adolescence, in part to explain the difficulties he had finding work during the early part of his marriage, in part to explain his anger at people he viewed as opportunistic antiwar liberals, symbolized by the professors at our local university. *Vietnam* in my immediate family was a symbol for masculine frustration.

But in my extended family, *Vietnam* was an actual place, an actual war where my uncle King nearly died. *Vietnam* was also the only time I ever saw my maternal grandmother cry. I had been conducting an oral history interview with her about her life in Seattle's Chinatown, and when I asked her to describe the happiest day of her life, she grew quiet, slowly bent her head to her chest, and began, silently, to weep. "It was the day Kingsley came back home from Vietnam," she finally told me, when she could manage to speak. I watched my grandmother wipe her eyes. Sunlight caught a wave of dust motes wafting through the living room, and for a moment they hung before her like a veil of tiny stars. For her, the terror of losing her youngest, favorite child was as fresh in her mind as the day my uncle had departed. My grandmother had not passed through that particular trauma, I realized, watching her. She was continually surviving it.

"PTSD is a disease of time," the anthropologist Allan Young writes in *Harmony of Illusions*. However, it is a disease of community and culture, as well. Writers at least as far back as Erasmus have noted that the violence and disruption unleashed by war last long after the fighting itself has ceased; researchers at the University of California, Santa Cruz, even found that the rate of non-negligent manslaughter and murder in the United States more than doubled during the Vietnam War. Foreign wars become domestic conflicts, violence abroad entrenched and spread at home. But if the theory of cultural trauma is correct, then where does the trauma end within a culture that endlessly promotes images of its own traumatization? How big does the traumatized community grow after a large-scale event—a war, say, or a terrorist attack, a wave of violence endlessly replayed on film and in news cycles? Are the Nguyens promoting our cultural narrative, if not our history, of Vietnam? And yet to even consider this argument would risk, I think, exactly what I am arguing against: turning a nation into a symbol for a precise reckoning of history that we cannot, or will not, write. To label America, or Kiet Thanh Ly, or the Nguyen brothers as victims of "the Vietnam War" turns real events and psychic pain into cultural symbols; it sanitizes them, it elides and overwrites them, perhaps ultimately it forgets them.

How do we talk about our traumas without turning them into clichés? Over the months I speak with people, it strikes me how often we do that for each other, making the war feel more and more opaque. As literary theorist Paul de Man argued, our very knowledge of history is the result of a delaying failure of representation: perhaps, according to this logic, we might read traumatic events as metaphors for the inevitable failure of representation that written history represents. War, violence, genocide, rape: these are all disruptions to the story of progress we want to frame as history. But war, violence, genocide, rape are not "disruptions." These are not, ultimately, metaphors for anything, and the experience of those who survived these horrors can't be conflated with the difficulty we have in communicating them, a failure of representation built into language itself. And of course to reverse this logic—to suggest that a failure of representation is traumatic—is obscene.

In language, there is always a gap between what can be articulated and what has been experienced, and trauma makes this gap more dangerous to cross. One risk of identifying people as suffering from either transgenerational or cultural trauma is that we deny them agency. But if we deny or dampen the power of trauma's heritability, we also deny people the right to see their actions as having historical meaning beyond themselves. Ly's case and the case of the Nguyen brothers muddy these already murky waters between individual and collective pain, between passive and active agency. They disturb what science wants to prove: that there is an endpoint where pain finally resides, where it can be psychically authenticated, then quarantined. There are, I think, many ethical problems risked in using narrative as a way of resolving PTSD and spreading the past's traumas, and they are unavoidable. But perhaps that does not mean they should not be risked. If we "fictionalize" our griefs to make them comprehensible, we also make the suffering of strangers an actionable cause: we share in grief's burdens. If we risk miscommunicating trauma or including too many people inside the term "traumatized communities," there is a greater ethical risk, I think, in keeping people out.

Ly made the Vietnam War a metaphor because he wanted to be understood. And yet I know his pain can't fully be understood. I know that his wounds are not the same as his parents', that his crime differs from the Nguyens' and is the result of a unique set of disorders, and likewise, that the suicide of Diana's younger brother, Oliver, is its own tragedy, and not necessarily a continuation of the Vietnam War. I know all of this, and yet I have also come to believe that these people and events are not unconnected. They are not so much a collection, I think, as a constellation of individuals: each one linked in a burning cluster to all the others, not because there is an innate or unbreakable connection between them, but because it is our gift and our curse that we can see them together; because we are in thrall to our stories, and because we, too, want to find a shape in the heavens, we make one.

9 The first war movie I ever saw in a theater was *Platoon*. I was a sophomore in high school, on an ill-conceived date with a boy from a family far wealthier than mine. I think I wanted to impress him. So I chose the movie, and I let him pick me up in his father's gold BMW, and then I spent the rest of the evening in a fetal hunch, fingers clawed over my eyes. The violence was too intense; even the boy seemed shaken by it. The hardest scene to watch was the confrontation between Kevin Dillon's character, Bunny, and a villager accused of hiding weapons for the Viet Cong. I remember Bunny's blue-eyed glare, and the thinness of the villager: a man little older than a teenager himself who seemed either mentally retarded, stunned with terror, or both. Enraged by the villager's inability to answer him, Bunny feinted as if to hit him with his rifle, stopped, turned to leave, then turned again to lunge with his rifle butt. The man went down. Then came a prolonged, unseen beating during which all I would let myself focus on were the screams of a woman in the background. A terrible, wet cracking sound, and then I felt the boy beside me flinch.

"I've never seen brains come apart like that before," Bunny said, after he had finished his killing. "I mean, did you see his head come apart?" I peeked between my fingers. Thick streaks of blood ran down the side of Dillon's face. "Have you ever seen so much blood?" From the corner of my eye, I watched the jungle-tinted light of the film flick across my date's face, turning him slightly green.

When I think of that movie now, all I see and recall is Dillon. His are the only words I can quote, his the eyes I can still clearly picture. About the boy his character killed, I recall only a vague figure in blue or gray, the blankness of his youth, the slow and stupid register of his terror. The woman is only a scream. She does not even speak a complete sentence—only one long, unremitting howl followed by guttural sobs. It is Dillon's face and speech that fill the screen: his stunned excitement, and then the thick blood on his cheeks.

72 Perhaps I blocked the young man out of my mind. Perhaps his murder was never actually shown: violence is often kept off-screen to secure a rating or to shield the viewer from what she already knows. Regardless, something about that man's absence from my memory drifts back as I leaf through my studies. My attention to the Vietnam War has always been confined to the experience of American-born veterans, their images culled from *First Blood*, *Apocalypse Now*, *Platoon*, *The Deer Hunter*, *Full Metal Jacket*. These films were riveting to me as a young woman, because they were the first movies I ever saw that were explicitly critical of America. I understand now that this self-criticism is one way to win a war that has been lost: to rescue our moral authority by critiquing our involvement in the war. And yet, considering the scathing view that American cinema has largely taken of the United States's involvement in Vietnam, the omission of any vocal Vietnamese perspective—the source, potentially, of our greatest condemnation—is a strange absence. Ours is the struggle and horror that compels us, and if Vietnamese Americans like Ly are invisible, it is partly because the Vietnamese have been absent from American mainstream treatments of the Vietnam War. The American veteran, on the other hand, we have portrayed as everything from a baby killer to a guilt-ridden protestor to a broken hero manipulated by cynical politicians. Even the United States itself has been turned into a victim of war, as ABC's Ted Koppel suggested when he asked on a 1987 episode of *Nightline*, "Is the war in Afghanistan doing to the Soviet Union what Vietnam did to us?" In our movies, when the Vietnamese appear onscreen, they are bodies to be tortured, killed,

ogled at, purchased. Our supposed sympathy renders them passive and inarticulate, even as we portray ourselves as monsters.

In 2012, NPR ran a story attributing the success of the American nail-salon industry, currently dominated by Vietnamese refugees and immigrants, to the influence of Tippi Hedren. This story, popularized by the *Los Angeles Times*, CNN, *The World*, and other media outlets, recounts that it was Hedren's volunteer work in a refugee camp and her "long, glossy nails," which several Vietnamese women had admired, that paved the way for their future business success. Hedren, moved apparently by the women's interest, arranged for the women's training and licensure in manicure. In CNN's 2011 version of this story, the video opens with a shot from *The Birds* featuring Hedren's shining nails, followed by images of Vietnamese women studying to become manicurists at a local beauty school. "She gave me so much," says one Vietnamese nail salon owner, while the manager of the school, a Vietnamese American man, tells the cameraman, "Everything [Hedren] did back in 1974 paved the way for what I do."

I am reminded of this story by Mai-Linh Hong, the lawyer and writer turned PhD student who is currently writing an article about it. The Tippi Hedren story, she explains, is an example of the way we subtly transform Vietnamese success into a story of American largess. Rather than detail the ways in which refugees and immigrants grew nail salons into a multi-billion-dollar industry, she says, these stories focus on ways in which Americans enabled refugee business.

The same thing can be seen in the ways that previous news images of Operation Frequent Wind, photographs depicting the U.S. pullout from Saigon, have been turned from stories of abandonment to images of rescue. Mai-Linh cites for me a 2010 NPR *All Things Considered* series called "The *Kirk*: Valor at the Vietnam War's End" in which the USS *Kirk*, fleeing Vietnam, returns in order "to rescue the [South] Vietnamese Navy," as one former captain recounts. "We forgot 'em," he tells the journalist, "and if we don't get them or any part of them, they're all probably going to be killed." The *Kirk* turns back for the forgotten fleet, roughly thirty naval ships as well as dozens of fishing and cargo boats. Over the week, the *Kirk* leads these ships to the Philippines, where sovereignty of the South Vietnamese ships is transferred to the United States, transforming them, and all thirty thousand refugees aboard, into U.S. territory and subjects.

When I search for images of Vietnamese refugees on the Internet, the first to appear are the 1975 *Los Angeles Times* photos of Camp Pendleton, the first base in the United States to provide accommodation for Southeast Asian refugees. Once the repatriation site for more than fifty thousand Vietnamese, these photos by Don Bartletti, himself a Vietnam veteran, portray Camp Pendleton as a domestic playground. In his photos, we see women washing clothes, children skipping beside GIs, women standing guard over sleeping infants, and children playing in a dusty yard. There are almost no Asian men here, especially not ones in their twenties; we see only one elderly man taking the hand of a toddling child. The refugee experience looks familial, tranquil, almost fun. Bartletti's photos downgrade the trauma of relocation by focusing on the innocence of the children's pleasures on U.S. soil.

The Bartletti photos aren't unusual. Search for other images of Vietnamese refugees, and you'll find photo after photo of American GIs playing basketball with groups of kids, of boys gripping the hands of American soldiers, of crowds of children perched, rapt, before a television set. The children appear playful and delighted, the women serious and shy. Few look directly at the camera: the photos document them without their acknowledging us, as if we were spying on them from some secret place, to observe them in their new natural habitat.

If the ways in which we imagine refugees are based on the symbolic faces the media gives them, then Southeast Asians were infantilized or feminized upon arrival, turned by our cameras into victims of a war they themselves could never have fought. It was not an unusual strategy. Among the most powerful images of the current Syrian refugee crisis was the 2015 photo of Alan Kurdi, a drowned child, whose small head was turned away from the camera, his blue pant legs lapped by surf. The image aroused both outrage and sympathy for the plight of Syrians streaming across the Mediterranean to Greece, but the sympathy was not destined to last. Images of drowned or suffering children were quickly displaced by inflammatory anti-immigration rhetoric after the November 2015 Paris attacks, in which lawmakers on both sides of the Atlantic began to express fears that terrorists might be among the waves of refugees pouring across our borders. Not even the refugee's portrayal as a helpless innocent was enough to ensure sympathy in the United States, where New Jersey governor Chris Christie said he would not permit "even a three-year-old orphan's" entry into his state in order to protect his state from Muslim extremists.

The West has long displayed contradictory attitudes toward refugees. When Germans, Catholic Irish, and Jews fleeing persecution in the Russian Pale of Settlement began arriving in large numbers in England during the Victorian era, their arrival triggered a crisis and a national debate in a country that, for most of the nineteenth century, had had no immigration laws to speak of. The result was a conflicting mix of socially tolerant attitudes among the British elite but violently xenophobic sentiment among the poor, as British high society welcomed wealthy Italian aristocrats, while less-educated classes attacked poor Catholic Irish in the streets.

The immigrant as an object of ambivalence quickly made its way into the literature of the era, notably into Wilkie Collins's *The Woman in White*, whose sympathetic portrayal of the aristocratic

Italian-language teacher Professor Pesca is counterbalanced by the novel's other notable Italian, Count Fosco, the novel's villain, and a liar, scam artist, and possible spy. But nowhere is the literary figure of the immigrant in Victorian England more obviously reviled than in the character of Dracula, who arrives in Whitby under cover of night, having killed all aboard his boat, who uses the bodies of women to feed on men, infecting and killing whole communities in secret.

This image of the refugee as infector carries on today. In 2015, Poland's main opposition leader, Jaroslaw Kaczynski, argued to deny entry to Syrian refugees because they spread disease. After twenty-eight hundred Syrians were relocated to Norway, many Norwegians began wearing gloves for protection against illness. Across Europe, op-ed pieces express concern that refugees will bring everything from cholera to HIV, terrorism to political subversion, spreading contagious diseases and ideas not just in the makeshift camps but in the refugees' new nations.

"Unclean!" Mina Harker cries of herself after learning that Dracula has been feeding from her veins, and our fear of hosting a contagion, of letting it circulate and thrive within our urban centers, spreading out through the arteries of our institutions, grows more palpable after every real or imagined attack. Italian philosopher Giorgio Agamben characterized our perception of the refugee as "bare" or "naked life," as if the refugee was herself just barely clinging to consciousness, half dead and half alive, perhaps in her liminal state of agency expressing the will of some other "unclean" political force or power. Like Dracula, or like the figure of the zombie, the homeless refugee hovers between our ideas of human civilization and utter chaos. If we associate the refugee with disease, we also associate her with civic instability, as one person I spoke with about my research on Ly suggested. "We'll need a lot more police protection with all these refugees pouring into our country," he said, shaking his head, as if the crimes that Ly committed would soon become routine.

I was struck by this, too, during the reporting on the Boston brothers Tamerlan and Dzhokhar Tsarnaev, who planted the bombs at the 2013 Boston Marathon. "Tsarnaev Brothers' Homeland Was War-Torn Chechnya," reads one April 2013 *Washington Post* headline, implying that the brothers, incorrectly identified as refugees, imported their former nation's political hostilities along with them to America. The boys' birthplace made them inherently unstable, some reports imply, describing the young men as "athletic and aggressive," their flight from "the restive North Caucasus" and the Chechen wars the origin story of radicalization.

By seeing the Tsarnaevs as simplistic and unthinking reflections of their homeland's wars, we give them a subordinate status relative to native-born citizens, whom we invest with agency: they lack our own individuation and ability to make choices because, having rejected American values, they cannot reflect them. Or perhaps it was the idea of their flight itself that some found problematic. This is an idea that Agamben also addresses, arguing that the refugee's statelessness is fundamentally opposed to our belief that all citizens must be rooted, calling into question what Agamben calls "the original fiction of modern sovereignty." Lacking national protection and rights, refugees represent threats to a security that is itself, ultimately, a fantasy. As there is no nation completely invulnerable to the forces that would destroy it, whether arising from outside or from within, so too there is no ironclad protection or assurance that any state can offer its citizens. For everyone's protection, refugees must be repatriated and policed. The symbol of the refugee frightens us because it is precisely through his plight that we come to understand how fragile our institutions are, how we are all ultimately at their mercy.

I wonder whether the absence of the Vietnamese in our Vietnam War movies, and our carefully orchestrated images of "childlike" refugees in America were, in some part, meant to mitigate these fears of refugees: how could we reject people we couldn't imagine having power? Such images also reflected American feelings of guilt about the Vietnamese at the time, our sense of being directly responsible for a war that dislocated thousands of families. And yet this sympathetic portrayal also infantilizes them: stripped of home and law and voice—even, as in the portrayal of the villager in *Platoon*, stripped of mental capacity—the Vietnamese in these images are defined by weakness and need.

On the flip side, however, I can see that the adult refugee might be portrayed as a voluntary itinerant, an opportunist. This, too, has been reflected by our changing attitudes about Southeast Asians. When the first stories about Saigon's fall hit the news, Americans were frantic to airlift children out of the country: Operation Babylift, which focused solely on rescuing orphaned infants, was the first of our mass evacuations out of Vietnam. Soon after adult Vietnamese began to arrive, however, Americans complained that they were culturally "unassimilable," here only to take advantage of our welfare system. Four years after the first wave arrived, only 32 percent of Americans wanted to continue to accept Southeast Asian refugees.

If we imagine the refugee as a beggar, then his care is not our responsibility; if he decides to flee, then we may decide whether or not to provide him shelter. But this decision is always dependent upon his assimilation. In the case of the Tsarnaevs, many wondered whether the American dream had failed them, or whether they had failed the American dream. "This was the quintessential kid from the war zone," Dzhokhar Tsarnaev's high school teacher told a *Rolling Stone* interviewer, baffled at his former student's crime. "[He] made total use of everything we offer so that he could remake his life." One former classmate drew distinctions between the brothers' experiences, saying, "[Dzhokhar's] brother and family weren't really Westernized. But Dzhokhar was really integrated into our school community. He was a normal American kid." This perception of Dzhokhar as "normal" is what made, for many, the younger

Tsarnaev's crimes so shocking, for to be successfully assimilated and still reject our values was unthinkable. Even the young men's uncle told reporters that "somebody radicalized them" and that what must have provoked his nephews was the sense that they were "losers" who hated anyone else "able to settle themselves."

"Fuck America," Dzhokhar Tsarnaev scrawled on the walls of the boat inside which he hid from police, and it's clear that in the complex mire of self-hatred and projection, denial and rage in which he found himself caught, the most important factor in his radicalization finally was the United States; it was America, ultimately, on trial. It's not a bad impulse to consider whether our culture creates outsiders by disenfranchising those we make citizens, but there is more than a little hand-wringing in our agonizing over the case of the Tsarnaev brothers. Our interest in the Tsarnaev case is in part due to our conflicted feelings about our own nation: how, over decades of conflicts, we have seen the ways our government has politically affected and even imperiled the citizens of other states. As the literary scholar Yen Le Espiritu writes, the refugee is a symbol used implicitly to bolster our own self-image, to support the belief in our own legal, economic, and even moral superiority.

Whether or not refugees are innocents or opportunistic scroungers, in our collective imagination, we are the ones to offer guidance and protection, shelter and sustenance. And if we are responsible for the wars that create widespread unrest, that have sent families fleeing across borders, then our portrayals of these same people become opportunities to turn conflicts of American aggression into what Espiritu would call "good wars" that produce "good citizens." "Good refugees"—dependents who mature into successes on our shores— rescue our morally ambivalent actions abroad. If we guide and protect, if we shepherd these strangers on to a better future, can't we, like good parents, claim some of their success as our own?

In order to preserve some respect for humanity, I almost never read a newspaper's online comment section, but I couldn't help perusing those in response to the *Salt Lake Tribune* site's articles on Ly. There were the usual racist and anti-immigration screeds you might find following any article about such a crime, but some comments radiated a deeper sense of betrayal. When I speak on the phone to Mike DeJulis, the father of Tim, one of Ly's stabbing victims, this sense of betrayal is made explicit. As in the July 14, 2012, op-ed piece he wrote for the *Salt Lake Tribune*, Mike DeJulis insists upon Ly's sanity, admitting that he "[couldn't] rationalize [it] as the act of a crazy person."

As Mike talks to me over the hour, he returns to the fact that Ly selected his victims based on race and gender. Mike sees Ly as a cold-blooded killer whose act was a politically motivated, premeditated slaughter of Americans. Ly, he insists, had to have been "turned by radical elements." Who or what these radical elements are he doesn't know. "He fell into the trap of hearing all that bad stuff about Americans," Mike tells me. "He learned that by associating with elements that believed these things. The South Vietnamese, we *saved* them."

I listen attentively as Mike speaks, his smooth voice cracking with anger. It is not just that Ly stabbed innocent bystanders at a shopping center that enrages him; according to Mike, Ly also betrayed the trust of the nation that "saved" him. This, strangely, echoes the language hovering around the USS *Kirk*, Operation Babylift, and also the Tsarnaevs: if the refugee is a childlike participant in his own relocation, then "bad refugees" are unthinking followers of unknown "radical elements" that turn them. And yet we also worry that their crimes are rational, they themselves aggressive actors bent on sowing civic discord. Ly's mental illness, of course, absolves him of much of this. But in Mike's mind, when it comes to Ly's ideology and self-perception, Ly is a passive victim; when it comes to his criminality, however, he must be self-determined.

It's not fair to place so much critical weight on the thoughts of a father grieving his son's attack, but I don't think Mike DeJulis's feelings about Ly exist in a vacuum. If Mike is, like me, obsessed with Ly's refugee past, likely this is because Ly resembles our stereotype of the refugee: homeless and unclean, barely human. But Ly's refugee background also activates another desire in us. If we can't go back and win the war, if we have narratively exhausted our grittier portrayals of our failures, can't we reframe ourselves as humanitarians?

Still, I am struck by Mike's belief that somehow only radicals would have been able to "turn" Ly. Could he really not imagine there would be no reason for a man like Ly to be suspicious of a nation that inserted itself into his birth nation's conflicts, killed indiscriminately, allowed its soldiers to rape or freely father children with its women, and that then abandoned his family to the very enemy they'd fought? I am not suggesting that Ly's acts of attempted murder are justifiable or sane. I am suggesting that the way that we frame his attack, and the violent crimes of other migrants, highlights our anxiety about the refugee's potential disloyalty. In that context, a migrant's or refugee's crime—rather than being an isolated event, or even a historically contextualized response—becomes only the sweeping rejection of our values and privileges. Given the two choices we symbolically offer to the migrant or refugee—assimilated compliance versus radical agency—we naturally prefer that they choose compliance. Agency might mean not only civic disruption, but the possibility that the refugee could kill us.

It strikes me that if our story of successful assimilation depends upon the migrant's adaptation to our authority, as well as on his upward economic mobility, then Ly's story—his mental illness, his indigence, his violent criminality—defies that narrative at every turn. It is why, perhaps, so many of the commenters on local news sites deny even the possibility of Ly's citizenship or naturalization, just as so many pundits kept incorrectly insisting on the Tsarnaevs' status as refugees. Their crimes aren't the actions of those who would be American, who should, according to our notions of the model refugee, continually express their gratitude for being saved.

10

When Keltin Barney staggered through the glass doors of Smith's and almost into the arms of his former classmate, Jeff Nay, it was perhaps the only lucky thing that day that happened to him. Jeff had just left the cash register with a DVD for his fiancée when he saw Keltin stumbling toward him, his right hand gripping his neck. He recognized Keltin from a class they'd taken together at the University of Utah called, of all things, Nature and Virtuality. As Jeff watched his former classmate slide to the white tile, his chest and arms slick with blood, he quickly realized no one else would come to help. The blood seemed to root people in place, each of them trying to determine whether Keltin's wounds were real, or if this was all a horrible joke.

Jeff helped ease Keltin to the ground. He knelt beside him, taking up the belt wrapped around Keltin's sticky arm while looking into his eyes, urging him to breathe. "It's going to be OK," he kept repeating. Jeff knew it was good to make a shock victim focus on something other than the event, and that a familiar face would calm him. Keltin, he noted, kept looking out the doors to see if Ly would return. This worried Jeff, too, and so he hurried with the makeshift tourniquet. So far, no one had approached them, which didn't surprise Jeff. "In all the times I've seen things like this," he tells me during our conversation at a local café, "I would say this is the norm. Or not the norm, but it is an expectation."

"What do you mean it's an expectation?" I ask. Jeff shrugs. "I just mean that I'd seen a lot of surprising moments of violence," he tells me. Then he stops and looks at me. "I'd just gotten out of prison myself."

This was, in fact, the reason Jeff fled the scene so soon after the paramedics arrived. If he'd stayed, he knew, the police might run his name, new questions would be asked, and a potentially heated discussion would arise that Jeff wanted no part of. So after ensuring the paramedics had loaded Keltin safely into the ambulance, he turned and strode out of the parking lot, his hands and shirt spotted with blood. After that, Jeff would monitor the attack's aftermath on the Internet.

A little over a year before, Jeff had been incarcerated in La Tuna, a low-security federal prison in El Paso, Texas, for aiding an armed robbery at the Salt Lake City bank where he worked. Tall and slim, dressed in jeans and a black T-shirt, Jeff has a mane of dark hair just starting to thread with gray, which makes him resemble an elongated Colin Farrell, or perhaps the lead singer of a melancholic folk band. His thoughtful and soft-spoken presence makes it hard to imagine him going to, let alone surviving, a federal penitentiary. Jeff himself admits how unfit he was for prison life—"There are plenty of people out there that could make short work of a guy like me," he says—but clearly he proved to be a quick study, staying out of range of the white supremacist gangs that tried to recruit him, keeping to himself, all the while working with a prison counselor to come to terms with the effects of his crime.

It's Jeff who is able to give me the clearest sense of what a criminal like Ly would face in prison, and who also shows the most empathy for him. Ly, currently housed in a jail wing reserved for mentally ill prisoners, under heavy lockdown and supervision, is "certainly in a more violent place than I was," Jeff says. Because Jeff's crime was nonviolent, Jeff was housed with other mostly nonviolent offenders. But Ly, Jeff notes, "is a more disturbed individual. And putting someone who's already psychically damaged in a psychically damaging environment is not going to create any reparative actions."

At heart, Jeff's perceptions of Ly's possible treatment in prison reveal the central question facing our justice system: who or what is Ly to us, and do we believe such a person can be rehabilitated? Rehabilitation of course depends on agency and competence, and the law holds that, should Ly not be judged competent to stand trial by 2018, the six-year cut-off date for criminal prosecution, he would be civilly committed to the Utah State Hospital; ironically, in this case, Ly's fate would be much like another mentally ill Vietnamese

perpetrator of a violent crime. In January 1999, a twenty-four-year-old woman named De-Kieu Duy walked into the KSL newsroom in the Triad Center in downtown Salt Lake, demanded to enter the newsroom and, when denied access, took out a handgun, then shot and killed a woman named Anne Sleater, in the process wounding the building manager, Brent Wightman.

Salt Lake City has had its share of recent violent public attacks. On February 23, 2007, an eighteen-year-old man with a trench coat, handgun, and a pump-action shotgun entered Trolley Square Mall on 700 East and began shooting customers, killing five people and wounding four others before being killed himself by police. The shooter was Sulejman Talovic, a Muslim immigrant from Bosnia who came to the United States at age nine. As with Ly, Talovic appears to have suffered from a history of mental illness and possible drug abuse; like Ly, any motive for his crime remains murky. In a 745-page document published two years after the attack, the FBI reported it could not definitively conclude why Talovic had committed the mass shooting, other than to suggest that Talovic had often frequented the mall with his sister after they arrived in the United States, and that the place evoked strong memories of loneliness in him.

The report also stated that Talovic was prone to making outlandish claims to friends, such as having razored off a swastika tattoo on his forearm to explain the large scar he bore, that he was in the KKK, that he "hated black people" and "faggots" but that he wanted to "shoot white people like Serbs." Though he wore a necklace that day containing a miniature Koran, there is no evidence that religion played any part in his attack. Talovic clearly nursed a virulent hatred for Serbs, likely learned from his family history, but Trolley Square and Salt Lake City are hardly places where large numbers of Serbs can be found. If he imagined the people he was shooting were indeed from his former homeland, he made no explicit mention of it in his attack. The shooting seemed spontaneous, his victims merely passersby on their way into and out of a local mall.

Trolley Square is less than half a mile from the Smith's where Ly attacked Keltin Barney and Tim DeJulis. It is a mall where I frequently shop, oddly, even more so now that the place, years after the attack, has been rebuilt. A new Whole Foods has gone into the cavernous trolley garages, along with some yoga studios and a popular bookshop. Talovic's family has since left the States to return home with their son's body, which they buried in their former hometown, near Cerska. Talovic's father told reporters he was too ashamed of his son's crime to stay in the States. Possibly, he was also too afraid. Typical of the anti-immigrant response to the shooting is a video on YouTube claiming that Talovic shouted "*Allahu Akbar*" during his attack; Talovic in fact shouted no such thing. All the iPhone video captures is the watery ricochet of bullets along the polished cobblestone walkways of the mall, the sight of a cop and another man darting around a corner, their voices shouting in the distance for Talovic to stop.

When my father heard about the shooting on the national news, he immediately called. My father phones now after almost every large-scale act of random violence that makes the national news. He is obsessed with public safety, and because I teach at a university where students with legal permits can bring concealed weapons into class, he is convinced I put myself in harm's way each time I teach. My father has always been a homebody, but since the terror attacks of September 11, 2001, his anxieties have ratcheted up to a feverish pitch: he hates how much my mother and I travel, complains about our nonchalance in public spaces after dark. He cannot believe we don't see what he does: that even our most placid cities have now become spaces of psychic unrest and vulnerability.

Telling my father about the stabbings at Smith's was, I realize now, a mistake. Now he calls after he reads about any crime involving someone Vietnamese, which, since he lives in Seattle, happens a lot. Crimes like Ly's and Talovic's fuel my father's fantasy that we all are at grave risk of being attacked by mentally ill or foreign-born criminals. This is not, of course, borne out by statistics. According to a 2014 *New York Times* article, only 4 percent of overall violence in the United States can be attributed to the mentally ill. Most homicides in America are not committed by people with mental illness, but by those who own guns.

Immigrants and refugees are also not more likely to commit crimes, violent or not: between 1990 and 2010, national violent and property crime rates *fell* while the foreign-born population of America swelled from 7.9 percent to 12.9 percent, and the undocumented immigrant population tripled. Even the conservative Americas Majority Foundation published a study that suggested crime rates are lowest in states with the highest percentage of immigrants. Immigrants overall are less likely to be in prison than those from native-born populations and, when they are incarcerated, are imprisoned for immigration violations much more often than for violent crimes. Crimes like Ly's, like Talovic's, like Duy's are over-reported because they are spectacular, because they are rare, and because the perpetrators are either not white or not seen as American.

I am aware that, having decided to write about Ly's crime, I am contributing to a convenient misconception. I am aware, too, that racism makes it both easier and perhaps more satisfying to make certain criminals faceless, to unleash the full strength of our anxieties on people we have turned into statistics or cyphers, on whom we can displace our fears that Agamben was right: at heart, there is something fundamentally unsettled about civic life. To expand our gaze to take in all the many actual perpetrators of violent crimes means we would have to examine white men, too, and also women; we would focus on parents as often as on single men. We would have to admit that the problem was never a foreign contagion but one firmly rooted in all of our neighborhoods and homes. To expand our gaze to an accurate scope would be to admit the possibility that, at some fundamental and unspeakable level, each of us nurtures the seed of violence.

While I am not afraid of Ly's refugee past, he does represent two kinds of chaos I most fear: indigence and mental illness. His representation of my fears has made it difficult for me to see him clearly, even as I write about him. Part of this has to do with the fact he's been legally advised not to meet with me. But even if we could meet, I suspect I would merely retreat into disgust: I would shrink him to fit my diagnosis. Who Ly really is exists beyond all of that. The real Ly would come to life where we each do: in the gap between race, genetics, social history, experience, and science; he is, as we all are, an unmapped intersection between the general and the specific.

"To me," Keltin said when I asked him to describe Ly, "the man is just a *blank*." At home, I stare at the various photos of Ly on my computer. One Ly in a yellow, V-necked jail jumpsuit, thick black hair stuck in tufted clumps. One Ly in a maroon jumpsuit, his wide brown face tilted downward, his eyes focused on something below the camera. But the Ly I keep returning to is the one with his head reared back, a silver and gray windbreaker zipped up almost to his throat. The faint shadow of a mustache darkens his broad upper lip. He's smiling, or smirking, I can't tell. He doesn't look insane at all, but alert, cocky, almost as if he's about to crack a joke. The mug shots make him appear drab and anonymous, but this image arrests me. He stares out at me from the photo, relaxed, almost challenging. He looks, if I didn't know any better, almost happy.

11 The possibility that we may be killed at random makes us believe we should not trust each other, a fear only heightened by attacks like the shootings in San Bernardino or Orlando, which fortify an inherent mistrust in our government's ability to protect us. But we are also enamored of these random crimes in our American mythos: they speak to a fundamental paranoia and perhaps excuse our own attraction to retributive violence. They are the crimes that lead us, as the journalist Bruce Shapiro argued in his article "One Violent Crime," to support a "Rambo justice system" that values punishment over prevention, vigilantism over social services. Shapiro himself writes from the perspective of a victim of violent crime. In 1994, he was among seven people stabbed in a coffee shop in New Haven, Connecticut, while having a drink with friends. The stabber, Daniel Silva, a young white man suffering from mental illness, attacked Shapiro and several other strangers after accusing them—falsely—of having killed his mother.

"The politics of [our] nation are the politics of crime," Shapiro writes, suggesting that an attack like Silva's or Ly's becomes a "Rorschach test" onto which we project our current fantasies about self-protection, violence, and urban life. The most virulent fantasy of these is, for Shapiro, that someone should have been able to prevent these stabbings. "Why didn't anyone stop him?" Shapiro reports friends asking after his attack, a question that suggests neither empathy for his wounds nor practical experience with crime. Such a question places the burden of protection solely on Silva's victims and witnesses who, according to this logic, should have displayed a "Rambo-like heroism," in which a single armed individual acts to take out a random attacker.

"Like Rambo," interestingly, is exactly how my father and the media describe another person who helped Keltin during his attack: Doug Duncan, an Idaho resident who, on the day of the stabbing, was in Smith's with his wife and two children to buy water and snacks. Next to Ly in the checkout line, Doug watched Ly fumble at the register, trying to unwrap a knife from its package. When Ly walked out of the store, the checkout clerk who'd helped him called out to Doug and his family, warning them that Ly seemed dangerous to approach. Doug had just exited the store with two gallons of water, leaving his wife and children behind to finish packing up the groceries, when he saw Keltin come into the foyer, screaming into his phone. Doug ran outside to find Ly confronting another young man with his knife, while a second student-aged man yelled he was going to call the police.

The student, Doug noted ruefully in conversation with me, at the moment Ly lunged for him, dropped his backpack to the ground. It was the one object with which the student could have defended himself. By now, Doug told me, he figured he was going to have to fight Ly off with two plastic jugs of Calistoga water in order to make it back to his truck, and so when Ly's back was turned, Doug dashed across the lot, dumped the water, and fished his gun out from beneath the seat. He then walked back to where Ly was attacking yet more men, circling slowly while his mind raced, trying to get Ly in his sights without any other shoppers stepping between them.

My father, when he calls Doug Duncan a "Rambo," is being tongue-in-cheek. But he is also intrigued by Doug's confidence, the fact that when Doug approached Ly and yelled for him to drop his knife and lie down on the ground, Ly did. *Rambo* for my father is both a slight and a term of admiration. It does not surprise me that he would use it. With crime, we revert to metaphors of war: in the early 1990s we were fighting "a war on crime"; the police are "the thin blue line" between safety and chaos; criminals put the average citizen "under attack" or "under siege." With Rambo, we have another war-related metaphor, this one from our cultural imagination of Vietnam.

In *First Blood* (1982), the only Rambo film my father and I ever watched together, Sylvester Stallone plays John Rambo, a Vietnam veteran suffering from PTSD. Long haired and bearded, Rambo arrives in Hope, Washington, resembling not a patriotic war veteran so much as the war's hippie protestors, whom the town's conservative sheriff wants to banish. At least this is what the sheriff tries to do upon meeting Rambo, who resists, arguing that the sheriff's order to leave town is a violation of his civil liberties. When Rambo refuses to leave, he's harassed by the sheriff's deputies, charged with vagrancy, then arrested, sprayed with a fire hose, beaten, and finally held down and shaved.

The police's treatment of Rambo recalls his torture by the Viet Cong, and so Rambo violently regresses in a series of flashbacks that make him kick open his cell door, attack the deputies, and flee to the woods. There he wages war on the Northwest town with little more than a hunting knife and a bow and arrows, reenacting Vietnam on American soil until his former colonel arrives to make him surrender. By movie's end, Rambo is locked away in a maximum-security prison, where he can finally feel safe: prison providing him not only stability, but the familiar and violent camaraderie of his former military life.

When my father invokes the name *Rambo* to describe the actions of a Doug Duncan, when Shapiro describe our justice system as acting "Rambo-like," we recall the legacy of the Vietnam War: combat experiences that cannot translate back home, where the violence our soldiers have been exposed to can only be contained inside prisons. In *First Blood*—the first of many Rambo films—America repeatedly betrays its veterans and military, turning Rambo into a symbol of our culture's hypocrisy, in which we cannot reconcile our desire for freedom with our need for public safety, and so we sacrifice our soldiers, resulting in a long-running war not just with other nations, but with ourselves.

Sadly, *First Blood* was not entirely without some basis in fact. After Vietnam, the number of incarcerated veterans rose, peaking in 1985, when more than one in five inmates reported having experienced combat. Veterans suffering from PTSD were particularly at risk: by 1988, it was reported that more than half of these veterans had been arrested, with a third of this population having been arrested multiple times.

Rambo condenses a host of post-Vietnam anxieties into one body. If *First Blood* makes him a symbol of PTSD and the rage returning veterans felt towards civilians unsupportive of the war, after *First Blood: Part II* appeared, Rambo became a mythic hero acting out our Cold War fantasies, a figure so popular that *Time* devoted a cover story to the wave of nationalism that followed in the movie's wake. But Rambo is no simple jingoistic figure, "miserable when he's at peace . . . [feeling] truly himself only when he's on the rampage," as David Denby wrote in *New York Magazine*. What I remember from watching the movie with my father was how often Rambo was physically humiliated. Stripped and beaten, shaved and kicked, Rambo is continually brutalized. The Rambo movies are as much devoted to the torture and violation of his body as they are to the orgiastic violence that he can unleash. Rambo is both traumatized and emotionally repressed, masochistic and volatile, a visual hybrid of veteran and hippie alike. He's also, oddly, both American and foreign, as the savagery he deploys is meant to recall that of the Viet Cong.

Rambo is our metaphor for America immediately after the Vietnam War: a socially disrupted space in which postwar anxieties about repatriated veterans paralleled our fears of an inflammatory antiwar culture, its activism that helped radicalize both the women's and Civil Rights movements. Rambo symbolizes our suspicion that certain populations, once touched by war, can't be suppressed or rehabilitated. In this vision, there is no community for returning veterans to join because they are now inherently damaged: they become outliers to our world, bodies to contain, not repatriate. They are our antiheroes. In other words, the vigilantism that we think we admire looks a lot like the psychic and social instability that we fear.

Doug Duncan is not, according to these definitions, any kind of Rambo. Doug had no desire to shoot Ly, he says: he only wanted to make him choose whether or not to be shot. It was a decision only Ly could make, Doug tells me on the phone when I call, having tracked him down through a private detective agency, and it's a small but crucial distinction. When police asked Doug afterwards why he hadn't acted within his rights to shoot, the question shocked him. "It disturbed me that these guys were trained to deal with this situation, but they thought so differently about protection than I did," he tells me. "I think it's sad that it gets to the point where sometimes an officer is so afraid of his environment that he feels he has to go to maximum force, and not deal with that force as it ramps up." That, after all, was exactly what Doug had done with Ly. Doug never shot because, as he told the police afterward, there was no reason to. "I told the police, [Ly] did everything I asked him to do."

It is perhaps exciting, even romantic, to imagine that some violent event will activate the hero within each of us. But Doug doesn't sound as proud of his act as I imagined that he'd be. Doug has a strong sense of responsibility to take care of himself and those around him; perhaps because of this he is soft-spoken and extremely clearheaded about the responsibilities of gun ownership. Doug grew up target shooting with his father, who gave Doug at age twelve the same rifle he had received from his own father. As a child, Doug carried a pocketknife his grandfather had given him, a gift that came with it the advice that he should always have the tools with him to be prepared, and so Doug grew up believing—for no reason that he can now articulate to me—that one day he would be called upon to defend himself.

Doug has spent his life thinking about preparation and self-defense, training himself to be comfortable and capable with guns, and when he thinks about the training the average person with a concealed weapons permit receives—roughly four hours of lecture on a gun owner's legal rights, with little to no shooting practice—he shudders to consider how many armed people have been poorly prepared. In many ways, Doug Duncan is the ideal gun owner to have been present in the Smith's parking lot that day, and still his actions did not come without a cost. At work, he was praised for intervening in the attack, then scolded for carrying a gun, something explicitly against company policy. At home, weeks after the event, Doug or his wife would wake in the night, rousing the other to talk. Though his wife had worked in law enforcement herself, neither she nor Doug quickly processed the impact of the crime. It took some time for Doug to make all the pieces of that day, and his former training, fit together, to let him see how his life had helped prepare him for the actions that he took. When Doug returned to Salt Lake a year later to help film the Tour of Utah, he revisited the site, in part to put any final questions he might still have about the crime to rest. Alone, he walked the Smith's parking lot perimeter, trying to see how his memories matched up with the space. People drifted in and out of the store, carrying bags, talking, laughing. Doug wandered past the store's glass entrance, feeling his head spin. It was weird how small the lot looked compared with his memories of it, how enormous the distance he'd had to dash across had seemed, and so he stopped and sat on the low wall he'd waited on for the police to find him after they'd handcuffed Ly, taking it all in. For a long while, Doug stared at the blacktop, bemused by the banality of the place, trying to remember what he'd felt that day, trying to understand why the stabbing had happened at all.

While 10 percent of all current inmates on death row are veterans, as well as 8 percent of all inmates in state and federal prisons and in local jails, these numbers represent a major decline in the incarcerated veteran population from the late 1970s and early 1980s, when 24 percent of all prisoners were military veterans. Currently, it is not veterans who constitute the most significant prison population. Instead, the National Institute of Corrections website states that people with mental illnesses are overrepresented in both probation and parole populations, at rates two to four times that of the general population. In New York City alone, a third of those admitted to jail receive care for mental illness, and as of April 2015, those suffering from mental health problems make up nearly 40 percent of the population at Rikers Island; there are more mentally ill inmates at Rikers Island than adult patients in New York State psychiatric hospitals combined. Even in Utah, county jails and state prisons have become "de facto warehouses" for the mentally ill, a fact that has been one of the driving forces behind moving the Utah State Prison from Draper to the west side of Salt Lake City: the prison needs more space to house mentally ill prisoners.

Shapiro, in "One Violent Crime," points out that the omnibus crime bill signed into law by President Clinton in 1994, with its "Rambo-style justice" model, would have done nothing to prevent the stabbing he endured. Indeed, Shapiro argued, the 1994 federal crime bill, along with a dramatically slashed national mental health funding budget and the subsequent shuttering of mental health housing and treatment facilities, only added to the likelihood of such an attack happening. In that, I can't help but see one more parallel between the crime that Shapiro experienced and Ly's attack. Although currently one in seventeen people in America lives with a serious mental illness such as schizophrenia, bipolar disorder, or major depression, between 2009 and 2011, Congress voted to cut non-Medicaid state mental health spending by 1.8 billion dollars. Even deeper cuts occurred the following years, impacting community and hospital-based psychiatric care, including housing and access to medications. Between 2011 and 2012, when Ly could be found assaulting medical health workers, joyriding, and abusing drugs, Utah's own spending on mental health dropped from 91 to 85 million dollars: because Utah refused Medicaid, which would have covered treatment for some of the mentally ill population, the additional 6 million dollar loss even more drastically hurt Utah's efforts to care for the mentally ill. Ly's attack can thus be seen through the lens, not of trauma and war, but of the United States's treatment of the mentally ill.

We might think that the mentally ill offenders in prison are all like Ly or Duy, but Jeff Nay's depression was a major factor in his decision to participate in his crime of bank robbery: in that sense, we must consider Jeff, too, a mentally ill offender. For Jeff, in-prison counseling and time to focus on his crime helped to heal him. But reparation and rehabilitation may be impossible for those suffering from schizophrenia or psychosis, and punishments such as solitary confinement become arbitrary attempts to isolate difficult people rather than working to rehabilitate them. Violence in prison is a fact of life: under its harsh conditions, many mentally ill prisoners deteriorate. In that, there may be one more sad parallel between the narrative of the returning veteran and that of the mentally ill. To put a man like Ly or a Rambo behind bars may be legally right, but morally questionable, in that it will also put him in a place where he can commit more violence on those Jeff wryly calls "people society doesn't consider assets."

At the word "assets," I can't help but think back to my father and his time in the Air Force. "The only thing I regretted about my service," he told me once in college, "was coming home." What my father meant was that he returned to a world he felt had grown unstable. My father, though he served during the Vietnam War, though he has worn a cloisonné American flag pin on his lapel since the terrorist attacks of September 11, 2001, is not an unthinking nationalist. He is simply afraid that something terrible will happen to me, to my mother, and that no one can help us or stop it. My father worries that the America of his childhood is gone, and it is, and perhaps this makes him feel increasingly vulnerable, and alone. As a young, white, educated man, my father believed the American dream was possible for him, especially if he worked hard, and devoted himself to his country. But the jobs didn't come through, his ambitions faltered, and he found no sense of camaraderie in civilian life equal to what he had experienced in the military. Over time, my father realized that he, like many people in this country, had been left on his own. Naive as his early expectations might make him seem, my father at age twenty-nine was unprepared to re-enter a nation whose ideologies had shifted so radically during his service. If there is a positive aspect to war, it may be the shared sense of purpose and the affinity it gives its young combatants, a creed based on unity rather than division. By contrast, for years after his service, back at home, my father felt himself adrift.

When I asked Jeff Nay what it was like to return home after prison, he told me only how he learned that he'd been released. After a year and a half in La Tuna, Jeff had been transferred to the county jail, but had no idea which date he'd get out. On the day of his release, he'd been dozing in his cell, startling awake only when his name was announced over the loudspeaker. Two guards came in and gave him a pair of khaki pants and a white T-shirt. After he dressed, they led him out. At the time, Jeff weighed no more than 130 pounds, though he is six foot two. He hadn't been eating in jail because he didn't move much: he was depressed, he knew, and scared of gaining weight on the junky food they fed him. As he was led out down the hall, the sight of his near-translucent skin in a mirror shocked him. He hadn't seen the sun in six months.

The corrections officers hadn't let Jeff call anyone from jail, and so alone, without a phone or money, Jeff sat outside the jail on the lawn and watched the sun rise in the sky, waiting until he could find someone with a cell phone they'd let him borrow, so he could leave a message on his mother's voice mail to tell her she could pick him up. Evidently, the jail hadn't notified anyone in his family about his release, either. After he made the call, Jeff lay back on the grass. It was cool, and his back and legs felt damp. Jeff closed his eyes and waited. He could hear the shushing sounds of passing traffic, a bird call, car horns. Someone was driving down the nearby road to get him, he thought. Right now. Soon, he hoped, someone would pick him up.

12

April 26 is the birthday of Tim DeJulis's son, and so Tim has gotten off work early to pick up a few things for Zane's party. Smith's is close to home, and Tim often walks there for last-minute groceries, birthday cards, supplies for the house. As Tim wanders through the aisles, the long shelves of red plastic cups and paper plates feel suddenly too bright: their colors vibrate under the fluorescence, prickling his senses, filling him with an intense need to slip outside. It's a headache, he thinks, squinting in the store's antiseptic light. But his desire to escape is too intense to ignore, and so he grabs a pack of plates and some napkins and heads upstairs to the cashier, where after a few minutes he finds himself blinking in the busy parking lot. The world is hot and white, and then suddenly it's not there anymore.

When Tim wakes, he's in a hospital room flooded with light. He can see the sun, he can feel it warming one half of his face, and yet the room feels completely, utterly dark. He falls asleep again, and wakes to someone telling him about a surgery. His wife, Susanne, sits beside him, along with their fourteen-year-old son, Zane, and their eleven-year-old daughter, Sophia. Shouldn't they be in school? Why isn't his wife teaching yoga? He opens his mouth to ask these questions, but finds, to his surprise, that no words come out. The place inside him where language resides is blank, as if his brain has been scrubbed.

His wife, Susanne, is looking at him with the concentrated stillness that only the truly panicked radiate. Tim can't talk, can't eat, can't move his right arm or leg. The knife Ly used to stab him pierced nearly to the center of his brain, nicking the area where language and memory are stored. When Tim was rushed into emergency surgery, Susanne told him over the phone, "I love you, honey, we'll be right beside you," and Tim slurred back, "I love you, too, Mom." Susanne has no idea what the results of his surgery will be. Tim was stabbed over his left ear, requiring a five-hour craniotomy to relieve the pressure building up in his brain. *People only get stabbed in the movies*, Susanne thinks, and keeps on thinking, even when the detective takes her aside in the waiting room to explain what's happened. Susanne spends a lot of time with that detective, staring at his moving mouth.

In the neuro trauma wing, groups of people sit, bewildered. Tim's parents have driven down from Idaho to be with him and his family, and Tim's aunt Terry comes by with the kids after school. Sophie is quiet, like Susanne, but Zane is furious. He sits by Tim's father, hissing, "I can't believe anyone would do this to Dad." Zane's anger is fed partly by Tim's father, whose own vitriol seems, over the week they wait in the hospital, only to increase. Susanne often catches the two of them sitting together in a corner, whispering about hurting Ly in hushed, furious tones. At a loss, Susanne finally asks the hospital counselor to speak with her son away from his grandfather, and after a couple of hours with the counselor, Zane returns, flushed, but calm.

A group of Muslim women whom no one knows and no one has ever met before arrive one morning with flowers and food. Susanne and her father-in-law accept the gifts, blinking back tears. The women offer to pray for them, and Susanne and her family thank them when the women leave. No one ever sees or hears from these women again.

There are cards of sympathy and phone calls, so many phone calls. Susanne takes them all while Tim sleeps in his hospital bed, his scalp shaved and a thick black zipper of stitches winding from the back of his head up past his ear and around to his forehead. He slurs less now, but his short-term memory has evaporated: names and dates, the numbers and types of medication the doctors enumerate for him disappear as soon as they are spoken. Because of his background in engineering, Tim slides into using technically precise descriptions when simple words fail him. When a speech therapist holds up a clock and asks him to name it, Tim replies, "A mechanical device used to tell time in small increments." Every month now is

September, the only month Tim can say. This panics his family: Tim is a technical writer for an environmental agency. His job is words, and he is the breadwinner, and before his attack he exceled at writing complicated drafts in a matter of minutes. Now, in daily physical therapy to rewire the circuits of his brain, Tim struggles to recite how to prepare a simple dish of macaroni and cheese.

"No one but you is going to know what you've gone through," his speech therapist warns him. "And when you get out, you won't be able to talk to anyone in a way that will help them understand." Tim nods, not fully understanding this himself. But after the long months of therapy—learning to use his right leg again, mastering the fine motor skills that a five-year-old relies upon, all while enduring headaches that feel as if someone has plunged shards of glass into his brain's cortex—he understands. She means he's going to be lonely. Susanne, after taking him home from the hospital, will handle him as delicately as a newborn, and he'll behave like one, spending his hours sleeping and eating, occasionally sitting up to engage her attention. Over the course of six months, he'll develop and grow like a child, saying the wrong thing or making hasty and often poor decisions, stumbling on the stairs, acting socially awkward. By the time October arrives, he will be closer to himself, a forty-seven-year-old man, but he will still, Susanne knows, not entirely be himself. Still, Tim will be deemed recovered by the doctors and physical therapists, and released as suddenly back into his life as he was yanked out of it, never again to speak to the physicians he's grown fond of, that he has learned to trust.

This is Tim's portrait of himself three years after his attack. I am speaking with Tim and his wife now about his recovery, a process difficult for either of them to articulate. Tim clearly still struggles with his memory. During our talk, his mind drifts: he begins, but never quite finishes, answering my questions. Tim's thinking is mercurial, as are his emotions. When he speaks about his work, the way that words seem to pour from the computer screen in a flood he cannot stanch, the comments section of the website he's meant to monitor making his brain feel like an overflowing jug, he grows agitated, sad. He doesn't think he can continue with this work much longer, he says; it takes all day to write a single draft, and the idea that he may be fired or let go fills him with both hope and despair.

But the worst part for Tim is feeling that everyone around him, except for Susanne and his children, has changed. The people he was closest to at work avoid him, he thinks, and friends he once spoke to almost daily have retreated from his life. He has the strongest feeling that they resent him, maybe for not being like he was before the attack, he says, or maybe because his presence makes them unsure what to say. Only once has he himself remembered the attack, as a dream in which a man's blank face and wild black hair loomed before him, so close that he could see the man's dirt-seamed features and flat eyes. Then the face dissolved and he saw himself on a gurney, a pair of medics cutting off his blood-soaked pants. He could smell the blood, could feel the cold drag of metal scissors against his thigh. It is his only memory of that day, Tim realized in the dream, and after he woke, the dream never came back. Now, when he dreams at night, the people he approaches harden into slabs of wood and metal, doors he cannot figure out how to open.

The therapist was right: Tim's life is lonely. Two years after the crime, his son, Zane, still snaps at him when Tim forgets something simple, calls him a dork, angry to be reminded again of his father's vulnerability. His daughter, Sophie, won't walk to Smith's or Liberty

Park alone anymore, and never wants to be left by herself. Susanne herself seesaws between an intense desire to dissolve into the crowd in public places, and feelings of recklessness. Such a random attack might be, in some strange way, a sign of how lucky they all are, she thinks now. Maybe she should buy a lottery ticket; perhaps she could jump off a bridge and survive!

It does not help that over the years the trial keeps getting pushed back. Tim himself has no feeling about Ly or the trial other than a profound weariness that he has to endure what, to him, has almost nothing to do with him. Though he wants Ly to be held accountable, he wishes it could take place without him ever having to step onto the trial stand or speak to a lawyer or answer another email or phone call or letter ever again.

But for Tim, the hardest thing to accept is that he doesn't know exactly who he is anymore, because he can't quite remember who he was. For him, the crime has permanently disrupted identity and time: he has no story for the changes he's undergone, nor for the crime's essential absurdity. The crime and his healing afterward offer no narrative for him to follow, no transformational clichés to fall back upon other than a continual sense of bewilderment, as well as pride at his family's resilience.

For Tim, the trial and Ly's punishment are society's only proffered forms of restitution and psychic rehabilitation. The Utah Office for Victims of Crime has paid fifty thousand dollars to help Tim cover the medical and household expenses accrued during his recuperation, as well as the deductible for his antiseizure Keppra prescription. But Tim is constantly stressed; he feels that the only purpose of his healing was for him to go to the trial, to be put back into the workforce. There is no time, he complains to Susanne, herself busy both working a waitressing job and running a freelance yoga-teaching business, to sit for a moment and just *process*. He is meant to rebuild his life, a life that he feels has not just been cleaved in two, but partially erased. Who was he before? Who is he now and who will he become? No one has been assigned to help him with these questions, and he doesn't have the luxury of time or money to answer them on his own. He cannot tell whether or not Ly's attack is to blame for this sense of being deeply, permanently lost, or whether this is age, the awareness of his mortality. It has been three years since he was stabbed. He has healed, but he has never recovered.

In my examination of Ly's crime, I understand how much I've privileged Ly's position. But Tim DeJulis and Keltin Barney were injured, too; I have to imagine them apart from Ly, even though the way that we portray crimes often absorbs the testimony of victims into the histories and motives of criminals. In that, the way we treat the stories of victims of crime relative to the way we treat those of criminals may be analogous to the way we treat the postwar narratives of veterans and refugees: though the two parallel each other, we are more likely to hear about the rates of PTSD in American veterans returning from Vietnam, Iraq, or Afghanistan, than in the refugees who follow in their wake. But the refugee's and veteran's profile look, oddly, similar; both populations experience similar stresses upon their return or arrival in America: the disruption and collapse of family life, the difficulties finding work, PTSD, the stress of violence and resettlement. Their experiences twine together.

I was struck by this often in my research. In September 2010, a Cambodian grandmother in West Seattle named Sarouen Phan shot and killed her fourteen- and seventeen-year-old granddaughters, Melina Harm and Jennifer Harm; her forty-three-year-old son-in-law Choeun Harm; and shot her forty-two-year-old daughter, Thyda Harm. Phan then shot and killed herself. During the attack, she shot off more than twenty rounds of ammunition, trying, police reports suggest, to kill all the members of her family. Only Phan's teenage grandson and another young girl survived, by crawling out a window. According to reports, Phan suffered from schizophrenia and may have stopped taking the medications prescribed by her physicians. Phan had fled from Cambodia and escaped to the United States after her parents and several children in her family were killed in the civil war.

The Phan case, sadly, presages an incident that occurred only three years later in California on Veteran's Day, when a sixty-three-year-old Vietnam veteran named Anthony Alvarez shot his two adult daughters, Valerie Alvarez and Jennifer Kimble, killing Jennifer and wounding Valerie, all while Jennifer's three young children watched. Alvarez, like Phan, then turned the gun on himself. While no motive has ever been ascribed to the murder-suicide, Alvarez's son told papers that his father had suffered from PTSD.

What I find interesting about the reporting of both crimes is their formulaic structure: in both cases, the stories begin with a description of the body count, then conclude with an implied diagnosis of the criminal based on his or her wartime history. These gruesome stories appear to have a simple cause and meaning: because of the murderers' violent backgrounds, these crimes are treated as inevitable reflections of war rather than individual attempts to process war's meaning. Whether because we see Southeast Asian cultures as inherently traumatized, or because we believe that war only devastates, the crimes of veterans and refugees become implied examples of how certain people are unassimilable: war-induced psychic breakdowns follow wherever they settle. In the contemporary story of war and its long-term effects on us as a culture—a culture that includes veterans and refugees—the conclusion of this story is always death and chaos, a tragedy that replicates the original tragedy.

In this context, the only benefit to committing violence is that it makes you visible in ways that suffering with and from violence does not, which is at the heart of Tim's complaint about his life, post-Ly. Tim and his story have been erased by this crime, and his disappearance into Ly's story might mimic what people like Keven and Trinh and Diana, and maybe also like Ly, have felt with regard to the history of the Vietnam War. As the Vietnam War has been absorbed into our contemporary narrative, our attention focuses upon either the violent or criminal act, just as our attention with war focuses primarily upon the experience of soldiers. A war story—and these crimes have now been absorbed into, and themselves become, war stories—is not about civilians who endure violence. The stories and memorials we create around war do not honor the women who were raped, nor the children who were bombed, but the soldiers who died in service of their countries. And of course, there are no memorials for the grandchildren and great-grandchildren who suffer from a family member's PTSD. Our representation of war encourages us to tell and thus authenticate only a handful of experiences. For the rest, we ask them to forget.

In being asked to forget, veterans and refugees have one more thing in common: both groups must repress their pasts to re-enter civil society. And the easiest way to prove themselves healed and repatriated, as any American knows, is through work, through showing themselves to be productive, visibly thriving members of our economy. Interestingly, Tim tells me that this is the greatest pressure that he feels: the success of his recovery is dependent not on his ability to remember, or to strengthen his family, or to learn who he is after the crime. It is dependent on his ability to contribute, and in that, to reassure others of his health. It's what the doctors kept repeating throughout his physical therapy, Tim says. They meant it to be kind, thinking Tim would prefer to take control of his life rather than to stagnate or wallow in his injuries, but in retrospect Tim finds the doctors' insistence odd. Don't worry, they kept telling him over the weeks and months of physical therapy, your wounds won't hold you back. In just a few weeks, they promised, smiling, you'll get back again to work.

13 During my conversations with Vietnamese Americans, the issue of work came up often. I was particularly struck by this in my conversation with Trinh Mai, who worried that she'd pathologized her brother's unemployment, treating it as if it were just a symptom of mental illness, something to be embarrassed about or hide. But what, she said, turning suddenly to face her reflection in the café window, if she's just replicating America's narrow set of expectations for him? What if she didn't write off his unemployment and anxiety as signs of illness, but saw them instead as masochistic forms of protest, even agency? Returning to these questions, I find myself applying them to the problems that trauma and violence present. What if trauma and violence are not psychic breaks with history, but violent attempts to re-engage with it?

In *The Body in Pain*, Elaine Scarry writes that "whatever pain achieves, it achieves through its unshareability, and it ensures this unshareability in part through its resistance to language . . . Prolonged pain does not simply resist language but actively destroys it, bringing about an immediate reversion to a state anterior to language, to the sounds and cries a human being makes before language is learned." Violence, many of us are told as children, is nonsensical, nonverbal: it is the act of pain and the cause of pain that we retreat to when we cannot or will not articulate our feelings. Violence, according to this definition, falls far short of words, and if it has any rhetorical continuation with our discussions about or understanding of others' treatment of us in war, it can only be mimetic. Violence is not, in itself, an attempt to rework war's original history, to comment upon or counteract it. Violence cannot be a speech act. In most cases, perhaps in every case, that's true. But some part of me resists writing violence off as purely inarticulate. Violence may be the only language for some to rewrite the wartime narratives that they've inherited.

By dismissing Ly's attack as "merely" violent, we lose sight of the fact that he spoke through a symbolic context that everyone in the parking lot that day appeared to understand. His act of violence was not random but intentional in its pursuit of certain victims: in that, it contained metaphoric significance that extended beyond his own pain to the pain he believed had marked his community. If we relegate people like Ly to a symbolic identity—signifier only of a traumatized culture or a particular conflict—why should we be surprised when he speaks back to us in the language and through the violent racial characteristics that we have given him? Essentially, if he saw himself as the product of war, isn't it because we never saw him as anything else?

And what, too, if such a violent reversal is not just about writing his story back into our consciousness, but writing against the predominant script we've assigned him: that is, a man with agency, determination, even masculinity's traditional aggression? By engaging in violence, Ly becomes the person we cannot overlook because he does not fit our cultural expectations: he is not helpless, not infantilized, not feminized, not voiceless. His violence gives him back all of the things stripped from refugees in the American media. It attempts to seize control of his community's collective memories of the war, too: to insist upon the visibility of an experience that, out of shame, many Vietnamese Americans also want to ignore. In that, his violence gives him an identity in both cultures.

To discredit Ly as solely mad may be both psychologically true and also culturally dangerous, as this reduces him once more to one of the faceless masses that have for so long hovered at the fringe of our shared wartime histories. Ly's actions may be meaningless, but his life may be historically meaningful. To write off acts of violence as always nonsensical, and then to write off the person who commits these acts as merely violent, limits our focus to his psychological vulnerability. When we pathologize Ly, or Oliver, or the Nguyen brothers, when we collapse our understanding of Alvarez or Phan to a diagnosis, we shrink rather than expand our vision to more closely examine the structural forces—the institutions and political realities—that also nourished their violence.

If we believe that trauma can't entirely be communicated to others, then recounting scenes of violence is only an act of spectacle. But though I recognize, like Scarry, that some part of pain lies outside of what we can articulate, I do not think this means that pain overall becomes unimaginable, and that others can't recount that pain for a greater purpose. The wounds Ly experienced and caused, along with the wounds that Tim and Keltin are each compelled to live with, may by their nature be specific to one person and different from any other, but they are all also are attached to contexts we can trace. They are all, also, now connected to a larger discussion about the Vietnam War. From that standpoint, trauma and violence may not disconnect us from others, but jolt us into an awareness of our intimate relationship with each other. Perhaps that is the ultimate value of recounting and listening to stories of trauma: to admit our emotional proximity to the past and to each other. To remember, when everything about our culture asks us to forget.

14

In Paris, in January 1938, Samuel Beckett was stabbed in the chest and nearly killed when he refused the solicitations of a local pimp named Robert-Jules Prudent. At the trial's preliminary hearing, Beckett asked his attacker for the motive, and Prudent, shrugging, replied: "I don't know, sir. Forgive me." Beckett eventually dropped the charges against Prudent—partly to avoid the publicity, but partly because he'd also begun to find his attacker's honesty strangely likeable.

I have forgotten this anecdote from Beckett's life until Keltin Barney reminds me. Keltin, it turns out, is a devoted reader of Beckett and Kafka, two writers who plumb the dark absurdities of a world that offers humanity no clear understanding of or purpose for its existence. It is Beckett whom Keltin references when I ask about his reactions to seeing Ly again during his own preliminary hearing. Keltin recalls that Ly's defense was that he'd stabbed Keltin because he'd heard voices. In that, the stabbing could have happened to anyone, Keltin tells me, which is the same realization that Beckett had about Prudent. It is why Keltin—like Tim—harbors no resentment toward Ly. He just happened to be a white guy in the wrong parking lot on the wrong day, and any attempts to explain what happened in a more satisfying manner ultimately fail.

Perhaps this is the reason why Keltin found the handmade card he received from Doug Duncan's family in the hospital both so sweet and so delusional. The card had said the Duncans were happy Keltin survived. It was a miracle, they said, that Doug had been at Smith's that day to help, and God obviously had plans for all of them. Keltin, recalling this now, looks slightly exasperated at the thought, as he does when he recalls his father's request when Keltin returned from the hospital, which was for Keltin to buy a gun.

Keltin's friends, knowing his talent as a writer, ask whether he plans to write about his attack, and Keltin answers that he's always writing about it. Stories full of terror, stories of the absurd, stories filled with pointless and indiscriminate violence: these are the things he writes about now. In his writing life, he's obsessed by Ly's crime—by his memory, and the memory of his terror—in a way that he can't quite explicate or put to rest. Like Beckett in his plays about memory, Keltin is more interested in narrative rupture, rather than smoothly written autobiography with the rough edges of memory sanded down. Were Keltin to write about it directly, he'd want to sound like Kafka or Beckett, writing in a postmodern form that would show the crime as it is: a disruption that will never be assimilated into the rest of his life.

In Beckett's 1957 play *Krapp's Last Tape*, the sixty-nine-year-old Krapp reviews his past in minute detail, repeatedly playing two different tapes, which he made on his twentieth and thirty-ninth birthdays, respectively, playing one and then the other for himself, commenting on each while also making his new birthday recording. The play, though entirely spoken by one man, is actually a chorus of men haunted by the past, fragmented by an obsession that history can't be recorded, that we do not exist cohesively across time but only in moments of it, that our memory of the past continually disrupts our attempts to order the present. The play is a series of temporal layers: there is no one Krapp, but three distinctly different men in our imagination simultaneously seeing, recording, and arguing over one life.

In some sense, this is what's happened for Keltin, as it has also probably happened to Tim and Ly: each of them has an experience to which he must return, struggling over time to articulate it. Keltin and Tim specifically are asked to carry the weight of the crime by providing a narrative for their friends and families, something that might put such random acts of violence into perspective for themselves, and by extension, their loved ones. By doing this, they carry the burden of explication, and with it, too, the burden of retribution, since it is only through their ability to articulate what they've lost that friends and family can begin to frame their ideas of what should constitute appropriate justice.

Perhaps feeling the weight of all these expectations is the reason Keltin and Tim have resisted doing this. Because of the three, it is Ly—the one ostensibly least able to make meaning—who has created such a narrative. By attaching his story to the Vietnam War, Ly has shaped a story for himself that Tim and Keltin cannot or will not write, since, as Keltin explains, using Vietnam as a metaphor just overwrites a basic crime. For Keltin, there is something dangerous and audacious about using history like this, a kind of sideways crab-walk toward the truth that frustrates him more than silence.

But of course, looking to writers like Beckett or Kafka to find an aesthetic style that might express life's violent absurdity isn't much different. In the end, we are each caught searching for some model to shape and contain experience, a form that might also make us feel as if we are part of a larger community. If the pre-existing conventions make us feel invisible, that doesn't mean we abandon telling the story. We just look for a different form, another metaphor, that can shape our experience.

And Keltin himself admits he often finds strangely symbolic resonance, even humor, in what has happened to him. Only the day after he was stabbed nine times in the Smith's parking lot, his uncle—suffering in the hospital from complications caused by long-term alcoholism—died. Keltin, who had always been close to him, was unable to visit him before his death, but his uncle had thoughtfully left something for him to find: a gift, his mother said upon Keltin's return home, which she gave him many weeks into his recovery. Unknown to Keltin's mother or to Keltin, his uncle had over the years prepared a special box—a gift he knew his dark-humored nephew, the writer, would like. At home, healing from his wounds, Keltin opened the box. Inside were nine tiny little knives.

15 They hadn't eaten for a week. And so when Duoc Pham found the unexploded bomb in a corner of the jungle far away from the rice paddy their mother was working, he immediately ran to find his older brother. The two had been in the jungle that day searching for wood. It wasn't until the morning's thick bank of fog rolled off, burned away by noon's glittery haze, that Duoc caught sight of the bomb's copper band glinting beneath a tree. The boys rushed to dig it carefully out from its hiding place, Duoc and his brother cradling the canister between them, hurrying home with it before any of the other village boys saw them, and tried to take the bomb away.

Bombs were precious in the village: food was scarce, and unexploded ordnance could be sold, taken apart for scrap, or, as the boys themselves had planned to do, repurposed into several smaller bombs they could use to blow fish out of the river. For years, Duoc's family had subsisted on a diet of corn, yams, and small bits of rice. Duoc's mother couldn't get much more than this, in part due to the war, in part due to Duoc. In 1969, Duoc's mother fell in love with an American GI stationed in the hospital where she worked. At the time, she was a widow with a five-year-old son, born from a Vietnamese father who had died during the war. So when Duoc's American father was sent to another hospital, leaving before he learned Duoc's mother was pregnant, she could not risk taking her first child with her to search for an American soldier in cities under siege by the communists. Duoc was born in 1970, and after this, Duoc's mother left the hospital to return with her two children to her parents' village.

Duoc, being mixed race, was treated cruelly at school and at home. His uncles called him a bastard and gave him the family's hardest chores, while the other villagers told him his mother was a whore. To protect herself from the communists after the fall of Saigon, Duoc's mother had burned all the photos and letters she'd received from his father. But she could not hide her son. Duoc grew up, much like his older brother, whose own father had died before he was born, with no knowledge of the man his mother was afraid to speak about. The boys' mother worked in the fields with her brothers now, though she took home far less pay and food for her work. Her history with men had made her family position precarious, and so the boys slowly starved together, rooting in the garbage for leftover food or searching the river, gathering firewood in the jungle to heat their home. Once, his mother admitted to Duoc that she'd considered wrapping a small bit of rat poison she'd found into a rice ball, and having all three of them eat it together.

Duoc's family didn't know they could have gotten an American visa due to Duoc. News of that possibility would come later, after they heard reports of an American journalist taking pictures of children who looked like Duoc. The United States, they learned, would pay a certain amount of money for each Amerasian child that came forward, which they knew meant that the communists would take a long time processing Duoc's papers, in the hopes of getting more money out of the U.S. government. Duoc himself would have to apply twice to leave the country: once in 1983, then again in 1987, after learning through a cousin who worked in the county records office that his papers had never been filed.

Duoc and his brother survived how they could: the bomb they found, the first in over four months, was a lucky accident. Duoc watched as his older brother lay the bomb gently on the floor of their hut, running his fingers over the flattened end to find a widened seam he could pry open with a knife. Duoc's brother, as usual, was smoking. Though only five years older, he had the thin-chested, stooped look of one of their uncles, and the cigarettes Duoc found in his brother's pants pocket were likely stolen from them. Duoc watched his brother's fingers as they found the seam in the bomb. Then he plunged the knife tip into the crack and began to rock the bomb back and forth on the wood planks, scissoring down the tiny crack as if trying to split an oyster shell in two, the heavy canister groaning between his legs on the floor. If he could safely break it apart, they could extract the dozens of explosives inside and reconstruct them into smaller bombs. Boys had been doing this for months, some with greater success than others. A boy named Linh had died three months prior, his arms blown from his body when the bomb exploded.

The metal end cracked off. Slowly, Duoc's brother reached inside to slip out the round explosives, each one fist-sized and golden, like the roe of a giant metal fish. Flakes of spark drifted from his cigarette. Duoc pointed at them, and began to warn his brother who, when he opened his mouth to argue back, let fall the cigarette. It dropped into the open belly of the bomb canister, and fire and smoke began pouring out. Duoc's brother screamed for them to run, but Duoc grabbed the pointed end of the bomb and began to drag it with him, trying to get it out of the house. The bomb was too heavy. Duoc dropped it at the door's threshold, and his brother picked it up, heaving it. Fire scorched the back of Duoc's legs and shoulders. He turned, screaming, to see his older brother's torso and the front of his legs burst into flame, along with the doorway and part of their house. Rolling on the ground, shrieking at his brother, Duoc watched the roof catch fire; soon half their house was gone.

As Duoc speaks, I can hear the sounds of children playing in his yard, his wife unscrewing the top off a fresh water bottle before she offers it to me. Duoc is in his midforties, his dark hair short and his olive face seamed. Like many mixed-race people, Duoc could pass for almost anything: Mexican, perhaps, or Russian, Sicilian, even Nepalese. His large and spacious kitchen is filled with jars and boxes of food. His wife and sister-in-law sit quietly beside him on stools, as does his friend Cuong, a social worker who has offered to help translate. Duoc's house has a large, well-tended garden, new leather couches, a red temple to the gods perched in one corner of his living room. But Duoc speaks, and I am in the jungle, watching his brother burn, as I am also in his kitchen with him, drinking one of the chilled bottled waters from his well-stocked fridge. His eyes are tearing up and I can see he is there and not there, as well, and for the first time during my year of interviews I see what Keven means by "confusion": the sense of living not just between two worlds, but between two senses of time: the endless back and forth of memory that confuses, and elides.

With a Chinese American wife, and two American-born children who have, according to Duoc, "the lives of angels," Duoc has made a home among relative strangers: no one in his immediate family shares or entirely knows his particular and painful story, no one in his family has starved or survived war, no one else in his family even looks like him. I can't help imagining that this must make him feel both grateful and lonely as he tells me story after story of flight, starvation, cruelty, survival. How do you live like this? I want to ask when Duoc takes a breath, even though I already know the answer. He has to.

I am speaking to Duoc on the fortieth anniversary of the fall of Saigon. All day long the news has been flooded with articles commemorating the war for a nation whose attention has turned to a more looming crisis: the protests in Baltimore over the death of a young African American man, Freddie Gray, while in police custody. The protests have turned violent, and a city-wide curfew has been set. At home with my radio and computer, I flip back and forth between stories of refugees still making their way in a new culture, and articles about young black men targeted by police, shot or killed for minor offenses.

There is something insane about moving back and forth between so many stories of violence. Over the year, I've spoken with dozens of people, strangers who've allowed me a glimpse into their lives, and each time I've been filled with both embarrassment and gratitude. One person leads me to another and another, and though there is no longer a reason to keep interviewing people, I continue to do so. There is no one refugee, I keep telling myself, and so the more interviews I do, the more compelled I feel to do others: each story draws me deeper into the mystery that hovers behind Ly's crime. I have to take all these stories into consideration, I tell myself, even though I know this is impossible: there will always be more stories, more individuals, and fewer and fewer answers.

A friend suggested that I speak with Duoc after I mentioned in passing an article I'd read on the *Salt Lake Tribune* website, in which a man named "Brine Shrimp" claimed to have helped Ly during the weeks before his crime. According to Brine Shrimp, Ly claimed to be Amerasian, something Brine Shrimp went on about at length, suggesting that the traumas of being biracial in postwar Vietnam had led to Ly's later drug use, indigence, and violence.

I had heard similar rumors about Ly from those who knew him in passing. And though I do not know whether Brine Shrimp made this up, or whether Ly lied about his racial identity to everyone he met, I suspect he would not have been above making such a claim. If his Vietnam is partly a psychotic fantasy of war, one in which he is the victim of American aggression, aggression no different than that of the Viet Cong, then why wouldn't he be attracted to that other tragic figure of history: the Amerasian, war's biracial product, reviled on both shores? It would be in keeping with his sense of being a victim of larger cultural forces, trapped in a body that encapsulates both his Vietnamese past and his American present.

Amusingly for me, my discovery of Brine Shrimp's story comes hard on the heels of an article my father sends me, this one about a mixed-race Vietnamese man who's shot and killed a white man in

Seattle in what was, supposedly, an act of road rage. Dinh Bowman, a former child academic prodigy and the son of a Vietnamese refugee, was tried and convicted in 2014 of killing Yancy Knoll, shooting him through the passenger-side window of his silver BMW. Along with the link to this article, my father, as a joke, also sends me a link to a Reddit page he found on mixed-race children, showing the tagline, "What is causing talented young Eurasians to kill?"

"Eurasians have acute memories," one commenter posted. "Biracial people often live in challenging if not hostile environments. So over time they become susceptible to psychological disorders."

"It's because they can't fit in anywhere," another commenter explained. "They never assimilate. And their parents likely sold them a lie that they could be white. Their fathers are usually ex-military and so they've inherited that aggression, too. I am so creeped out, I'm going to stay the fk away from Eurasian guys from now on."

"Look, honey," my father writes below the link. "You, too, could become a criminal!"

Sighing, I shut down my computer.

There are, currently, around seventy-seven thousand Amerasians and their family members in the United States; according to Duoc, nearly two hundred of them live in Salt Lake. Those interested in tracking down their fathers can take a DNA test and have their results archived in a database to help match them up with their American relatives. Duoc himself took the test, but he hasn't used the results to find his father, afraid that his father may suspect that Duoc wants money from him, afraid, too, that he might make his father lose face with his wife and children, if he has any. Duoc wants his father to be proud of having him as a son, something he is not sure his father would be, regardless of his success. If Ly pretended to be Amerasian as way of symbolizing his tragic status, Duoc is certainly no tragic figure for Ly to emulate. Duoc runs a small business and has a large and now prosperous family; his brother survived his injuries and has joined him in the United States. Duoc works hard on behalf of Amerasians across America, even recently visiting Washington, D.C., to lobby Congress to bring back the final Amerasians still living in Vietnam. Only some part of Duoc carries a legacy of shame around his racial identity drilled into him from childhood, where his very existence reminded every-

one about his mother's past.

One poignant irony is that Duoc's "shameful" wartime identity is now something young Vietnamese appear to celebrate and envy. In Vietnam, images of mixed-race Vietnamese women and men grace the covers of popular magazines, television ads, movie posters. Strangers in my Ba Dình neighborhood often commented on my appearance, coming up to ask eagerly if I was "Asian peoples," then grinning at my answer, which caught me off guard. I'm the same age as Duoc: if anything, I thought, I should be a similar antiquated figure of cultural revulsion. Perhaps, I thought, my neighbors were merely being polite. But over my months in Vietnam, I began to see that it was my Americanness that allowed my racial ambiguity to be seen as positive, whereas Duoc would likely still be met with alarm. Duoc is Vietnamese: his fluency in the culture would make his racial difference appear all the more uncanny to strangers, threatening, even obscene. I, however, am not half-Vietnamese; I am completely American, obviously U.S. raised, and also U.S. born: I am an object that can be observed with equanimity, because I unsettle no one's ideas about what constitutes being Vietnamese.

When Duoc tells me about his desire and reluctance to find his father, of his sense of living between worlds, I can only imagine what this means. Though mixed race myself, I have never questioned in which country, in which time frame I belong. Though I recognize that in the scope of American history my biracial body is political, I also know it was not shaped by war. In that, I understand the deep historical luck of my position. It is a luck that Duoc, too, in America, has strangely benefitted from. If in Vietnam Duoc was punished for his biracial identity because he symbolized the enemy, in the United States he's rarely recognized as Vietnamese. Strangers assume he's Latino; Duoc's boss on his first construction crew even hired him because he assumed he was Mexican. Duoc has to tell people of his past for them to see it: in that sense, America, even as it has allowed him some respite from pain, conveniently represses what it doesn't think to observe. Duoc's ambiguous racial position here means that some part of his success on our shores was in part due to his particular invisibility.

Thinking this as I leave Duoc's house, I am reminded of a late night I spent, lost and alone, in Saigon. I had just left a crowded restaurant and got turned around on my way back to the hotel. On a street corner filled with shops selling plastic flowers, I stopped to dig out the dog-eared map I'd gotten from a friend. As I squinted at the paper, I felt someone emerge from the shadowy doorway behind me. I looked up and saw a man, older than me perhaps, with long and rough-looking hair. He was alone, I noticed, and he held the thin, torn flaps of his shirt collar closed with one hand. He did not speak to me: he simply stood beside me in the dark, like me, perhaps, waiting for a break to open in the traffic. I went back to my map but could feel him look at me, suddenly, hard in the face. I raised my head and saw his round, double-lidded eyes, the high cheekbones, his skin darkened by years of living in the sun. His nose and mouth looked just like mine. He stared at my face, then looked down at my jacket, my clean jeans. Something in the two of us shifted, recognized each other. He took a step back from me. Then a rift in the traffic opened, and I crossed.

16

We have memorialized the Vietnam War in stone and on film, in our political rhetoric, in gravesites, in metaphor. As a cautionary tale, Vietnam has been invoked not just by American politicians and war veterans, but by South African politicians during the Border War, by the Soviets when speaking about Afghanistan, by politicians across the globe arguing against engaging in wars perceived to be unwinnable. The Vietnam War is a story of loss, turmoil, trauma, division. As novelist and critic Viet Thanh Nguyen has noted, Vietnam is a war increasingly taken out of its time and context, and by enlarging this idea of Vietnam—by extending its reach across history and continents—we lose sight of its many victims and combatants. In some ways, the war itself is both invisible and unassimilable. We don't necessarily remember its specifics, even as we constantly invoke it.

"You killed my people," Ly cried, and when I think about the various meanings and people embedded in this sentence, it strikes me that, in ways both figurative and literal, he's right. If I read his violent acts as a response to history, then his possible pretense at being Amerasian may, at some level, act as yet another reminder of all the bodies that Vietnam involved. Vietnam was never only a war of American soldiers, but those of our Asian allies and foes, the children we left behind, the refugees we took in and sometimes let founder. The war moved through Southeast Asia, North America, Australia, Europe. It traveled across class and gender and ethnic lines, down through the DNA of generations. The Vietnam War was and remains a plastic construct, changing the way that collective memory around war always changes, adapting to the needs of the narrators at hand.

Even our ideas about "the wartime refugee" and the "veteran" marry theoretical language with sociological realities: in this way, refugees and veterans too have become constructs of economic fact and cultural speculation. Like the image of the Amerasian, the appearance of war and its many victims shapeshifts, changing its definition according to the person who looks at it.

The French philosopher Paul Ricoeur, who spent five years as a prisoner of war in a German camp during World War II, argued that we need an "ethical remembering" of history: a way of creating historical narratives that take into account as many individuals as possible, especially those who would otherwise be excluded from the record because of poverty, race, citizenship, illness, gender, or literacy. I suspect, however, that to take in all of these stories, to record them, and to remember them appropriately would be, if taken to its logical conclusion, impossible: in our attempt to memorialize all those that war touched, we would numb ourselves through the recitation of names and facts. We would lose individuation even as we tried to reinstate it. There is a reason we turn to metaphor, I believe, and that is because, try as we might, we cannot actually conceive of or articulate war's blinding totality.

That is not to say, however, that we shouldn't try. Ly and the other hundreds of thousands of refugees have no memorial on our shores. The Vietnam War as a metaphor has erased those we helped displace, those who have now become Americans themselves. In the crimes of Kiet Thanh Ly and in the happier narratives of people like Keven or Duoc may be the seeds of a new kind of memorial: not the stone facade of a polished monument, but the communal narratives and fantasies passed down through generations: messy, hopeful, contradictory, multivocal, even violent.

In 1984, two years after it was erected, I visited the Vietnam Veterans Memorial in Washington, D.C., where I was visiting with my family to attend my cousin's graduation from the Naval Academy. That year, my cousin was in the top ten of his class; he was also graduating as one of its only Asian Americans. After the ceremony, my parents, my uncle, and I all went to the Mall to visit the museums and the memorial. I remember a long line of people waiting to walk past its glossy black flanks, two planes of dark stone that narrowed then widened into an enormous V. My uncle wandered somewhere ahead, possibly searching for the names of friends he'd lost, possibly trying to get out of the crush of people walking on the black-bricked path. The memorial had opened only two years before, and the controversy surrounding it—no stone wreaths, critics complained, no statues of soldiers, the thing built by a Chinese girl with no sense of why this war was fought at all—was what attracted my family.

As a preteen, the memorial made little sense to me. Why would it? The memorial lacks an obvious story: only names carved in black, alphabetized and capitalized, crushed together in long lines so as to be almost unreadable from a distance, a faded blur if you squint your eyes just right. I squinted my eyes. People moved to the right and left of me. My parents pushed forward, the crowd breaking up as people looked for and found particular names, their fingers catching and dragging across the wall. My uncle disappeared from view. The woman next to me touched a name at eye height. Her fingerprints seemed to evaporate as soon as her fingers touched the stone.

Years later, in *Art in America*, Maya Lin would tell an interviewer that she'd proposed to list the names of the soldiers in the order of their deaths, "to return the vets to the time frame of war," she said. I am fascinated by that statement, by the idea that war's time—if represented correctly—might actually be timeless for those coming to it anew, that we could feel ourselves immersed in war's power: the past and present twined into one. Or perhaps I'm getting her meaning all wrong: perhaps time can be frozen, the events of the past locked in an order that is reproducible, but also static.

But memory disorders time, and trauma disorders memory. And perhaps that is the conflict about which Ly's crime most hauntingly reminds me: that if healing depends upon the ordering of our memories, on the reconstruction of time through a narrative that we create, the very fact of war and its trauma makes this impossible. To heal we need to express what cannot be expressed, because it stands against catharsis and conclusion, because it defies meaning. Our national monuments and museums memorialize trauma through odes to institutional power, death, and loss, but they do not always ask us to consider ourselves as part of the story we tell about loss. Monuments are locked into time in ways that culture, which changes, isn't. A monument tells us war is over. But everything about the ways that we process war suggests it never is.

When I think about visiting the Vietnam Veterans Memorial, I remember feeling mostly boredom. I was tired from the heat and suffering from allergies. I was also a little shaken by what I'd overheard someone say at my cousin's graduation ceremony. "Did you get a look at that Oriental up on stage?" a man had muttered as I passed by, his sunburned wife turning her head at the question, a small grimace twitching her lips. I don't think they saw me listening to them, and of course, if they had, they wouldn't have recognized me as Jon's cousin. They probably wouldn't even have thought I was Asian.

At the memorial, I wondered whether to bring up the man's question with my parents but chose not to. Still, I was distracted, trying to understand the exact meaning of that sentence, the wife's grimace. I didn't think to look too carefully at my uncle as he strolled alone along the wall, or at my father, who stood with my mother to one side, an expression of something like relief flickering across his face. At my cousin's graduation ceremony, I didn't think to look too closely at my cousin Jon, either, handsome in his Navy whites, not knowing that seven years later he would be on the U.S. submarine that would launch our first wave of missile strikes against Baghdad: George H. W. Bush's "shock and awe" campaign, which I would later drunkenly watch on television with college roommates, shouting obscenities as the grainy flares lit up our screen. I didn't know that seventeen years later, on September 11, 2001, when American Airlines flight 77 crashed into the Navy wing of the Pentagon, Jon would lose dozens of his friends and colleagues and narrowly miss dying himself, stuck in heavy traffic on his way back to the Pentagon from Langley.

Looking back, I can dig through these memories to find, or perhaps just to create, the relevant images in which my family's story was unfolding. My uncle pausing at the wall, peering at a name. My cousin turning at our shouts when his name is called, the flash of my mother's camera washing him out. But what am I to make of these stories all together? How, when war turns into war turns into war, am I to find its final resting place?

When Mike DeJulis wrote in his op-ed piece for the *Salt Lake Tribune* that the Vietnam War had nearly taken two more casualties, he was partly right. If we consider Ly another near-casualty of war, we must add him to the list, too, along with his family, along with the families of Tim DeJulis and Keltin Barney, and even Jeff Nay and Doug Duncan. In essence, this new and growing constellation of victims continues to shift and rearrange. Three and a half years after his 2012 stabbing, Kiet Thanh Ly has finally been judged competent to stand trial. In September 2015, he pled guilty to two counts of attempted murder. Prosecutors dropped the additional charges of aggravated assault and recommended that, prior to prison, Ly receive treatment at the Utah State Hospital. On November 18, 2015, the judge agreed, and Ly was sentenced to two terms of three years to life in prison. The sentences will run concurrently.

I missed the trial. The date had changed so many times since Ly was first charged that I skipped it, assuming that this court date would be, like all the others before, a waste: even his lawyer thought that Ly might never qualify as competent. To our surprise, we were wrong. After Ly was sentenced, I read about it on the Web via links that friends sent me. The *Salt Lake Tribune*, for a day, ran the outcome in the back pages of the local section of the paper. Then the trial was forgotten, the outcome treated as another nonstory. The trial's conclusion may bring some kind of relief for Keltin, Tim, and their families, but for most people the trial will only become another and thankfully minor spectacle caused by a mentally disturbed foreigner, desperate to blame his personal problems on a war.

Perhaps it is laughable to investigate such a small case, one that itself has little national importance, which has generated so little newsworthy commentary. But when Prudent stabbed Samuel Beckett, as Keltin reminds me, it was not that Prudent's act, by itself, had meaning or social importance. Prudent's random attack became for Beckett proof that the universe must be fundamentally irrational: Beckett learned to see his world anew in part because of Prudent's attack. When we say that Ly is crazy or not conscious of his actions, these facts may be beside the point. I believe that Ly can teach us something about the war that he—and we—are still struggling to articulate.

When I visited the Vietnam Military History Museum all those times in Hanoi, why didn't I ever touch the planes? There was no fence surrounding the monument, no signs telling me not to handle or even climb the sculpture. But no one touched it, no matter how close each of us got to look at it, to photograph or draw it, as I saw one young woman do during a lunch hour. Perhaps awe or inculcated respect for public art kept us polite, gazing at the wreckage from our safe periphery. Or perhaps it was too grotesque to imagine touching. At some point, the planes became synonymous with bodies for me, my grief and awe and anger for those that died transferred onto the crumpled sheet of each metal wing. To touch even one piece would be, I thought, a transgression, like stroking the face of a dead stranger.

In retrospect, I should have touched it. The monument had made war material to me: it treated time and history roughly, layering the French planes beneath and between the American ones, mixing up the conflicts with little regard for historical accuracy. The accuracy, I saw, was entirely in the fact of the planes. They were all the evidence that mattered: the dates of the battles, the specificities of the conflicts, the identities of the pilots themselves meant, beside this wreckage, almost nothing. We were meant to see these wars as one continuous narrative, the monument showed me, to see their violence bringing together multiple combatants, diverse victims into one shattered body.

Why did I preserve such reverence for a monument that demanded, through its very construction, its gross physicality, the gut-punch recognition of my vulnerability, my physical presence beside its physical presence? I was already part of the sculpture. If we think of a war memorial not as a static event but a process, an endless retelling—much like the way that trauma itself is and requires a retelling—then we are all part of the memorial. Our true monument is not the Vietnam Veterans Memorial's black wings of stone, it is not even the names carved in the stone. It is my uncle standing at the wall, a little apart from us, touching a name I can't read. Or rather, the moment before he touches it: that space between his hand and the stone, where he reaches for—but cannot yet meet—the wall's dark, reflective face.

NOTES AND SELECTED SOURCES

To list or comment on all the articles and books consulted for this project would extend this section too much in length, so the notes below include only specific works cited and some of the more important additional sources. This book relies heavily upon interviews conducted with Keltin Barney, Tim DeJulis, Mike DeJulis, Doug Duncan, Susanne Gipson, Mai-Linh Hong, Keven Lee, Jeff Nay, Trinh Mai, Cuong Nguyen, Diana Khoi Nguyen, Linh Nguyen, Duoc Pham, Diana Phong, Plum Schultz, and oral interviews from the University of Utah American West Center's *Saving the Legacy: An Oral History of Utah's Veterans* archive.

8   *outlines of the crime*   Information about Kiet Thanh Ly's crime comes from the following: Andrew Wittenberg et al., "Man Buys Knife, Stabs 2 at Salt Lake City Store," *KSL.com*, April 26, 2012; Ben Winslow et al., "Concealed Weapons Permit Holder Stops Parking Lot Stabbing," *Fox 13 SLC News*, April 26, 2012; Pat Reavy, "Suspect in Stabbing Has Long Criminal History," *Deseret News*, April 27, 2012; Nate Carlisle, "Suspect in Salt Lake City Store Stabbings Jailed a Week Earlier," *Salt Lake City Tribune*, April 27, 2012; Lori Pritchard, "Victim of Stabbing Talks about Experience," *KSL.com*, April 30, 2012; Erin Alberty et al., "Man Charged with Stabbing Two Outside Grocery Store," *Salt Lake City Tribune*, April 30, 2012; Lori Pritchard, "Stabbing Victim Thankful for Kindness of Passersby," *Deseret News*, May 1, 2012; Aaron Falk, "Man Charged in Salt Lake City Grocery Store Stabbing Appears in Court," *Salt Lake City Tribune*, May 3, 2012; "Man Accused in Grocery Store Stabbings Appears in Court," *FOX 13 SLC News*, October 18, 2012. Information about Ly's prior police record comes from court documents provided by the Salt Lake County Courthouse.

18   *"ethnic enclaves"*   On "ethnic enclaves," see Tuyen Ngoc Tran,
      "Behind the Smoke and Mirrors: The Vietnamese in California,
      1975–1997" (PhD diss., University of California, Berkeley, 2007),
      81. Some also feared that heavy concentrations of refugees would
      exacerbate "areas of high unemployment, housing shortages, and
      overburdened welfare cases." See U.S. General Accountability Office,
      The Indochinese Exodus: A Humanitarian Dilemma (Washington, D.C.:
      GPO, 1979), accessed November 29, 2016, http://gradworks.umi
      .com/33/06/3306370.html.

18   *more than nine hundred thousand refugees*   James W. Tollefson,
      "Indochinese Refugees: A Challenge to America's Memory
      of Vietnam," in *The Legacy: The Vietnam War in the American
      Imagination*, ed. D. Michael Shafer (Boston: Beacon Press, 1990),
      262. Information about the number of refugees that were repatri-
      ated to the United States post-1990 comes from the U.S. General
      Accountability Office, Representative Anh Cao, *H. Res. 1331:
      Recognizing and Appreciating the Historical Significance and the Heroic
      Struggle and Sacrifice of the Vietnamese People and Commending the
      Vietnamese-American Community and Nongovernmental Organizations*
      (Washington, D.C.: GPO, 2010) accessed November 23, 2016, https
      ://www.congress.gov/bill/111th-congress/house-resolution/1331
      /text; and the United Nations High Commissioner for Refugees
      (UNHCR), "Flight from Indochina," in *State of the World's Refugees
      2000: Fifty Years of Humanitarian Action*, UNHCR, accessed November
      23, 2016, http://www.unhcr.org/en-us/publications/sowr/3ebf9bad0
      /state-worlds-refugees-2000-fifty-years-humanitarian-action
      -chapter-4-flight.html.

18   *from Vietnam, Laos, and Cambodia*   Information in this chapter
      about the refugees and about Vietnam in general after the departure
      of the United States is taken from oral histories and from the UN
      High Commissioner for Refugees, "Flight from Indochina," in *State
      of the World's Refugees 2000*, 83–87.

20   *refugees out in the tens of thousands*   "Flight from Indochina," in
      State of the World's Refugees 2000, 83.

21   *exact number of people*   Cao, *H. Res. 1331.*

22   *employment on production lines*   Carol Edison, "Southeast Asian History," in *Utah History Encyclopedia*, accessed November 16, 2016, http://www.uen.org/utah_history_encyclopedia/s/SOUTHEAST _ASIANS_IN_UTAH.html.

22   *divisive, materialistic, conformist, even classist*   From oral histories taken in interviews with Cuong Nguyen, Diana Phuong, Trinh Mai, and Keven Lee.

23   *a double blow*   For this formulation, see Jean-François Lyotard, *Heidegger and "the Jews,"* trans. Andreas Michel and Mark S. Roberts (Minneapolis: University of Minnesota Press, 1990), 16. Freud's thinking about trauma evolved over time and informed many of his major texts, beginning with the early *Studies on Hysteria* (1895). I draw primarily on *Mourning and Melancholia* (1917) and *Beyond the Pleasure Principle* (1920) and on later scholars, such as Cathy Caruth, Dori Laub, and others, who have extended Freud's thinking.

23   *Post-traumatic stress disorder*   The description of post-traumatic stress disorder symptoms is variable and, among psychiatrists and critics, contestable. For an overview, see Judith Shulevitz, "The Science of Suffering," *New Republic*, November 16, 2014, accessed November 29, 2016, https://newrepublic.com/article/120144 /trauma-genetic-scientists-say-parents-are-passing-ptsd-kids.

23   *trauma becomes the body's default setting*   The controversy surrounding PTSD as a diagnosis stems partly from the wide variety of its symptoms. On top of this, some psychiatrists and researchers argue that PTSD is both a culturally determined phenomenon and a medical one. According to David J. Morris, there is a "storytelling problem" associated with PTSD. "Specifically," he asks, "what cultural narratives are available to a returning veteran?" Cultural narratives ensure that different nations' soldiers are diagnosed differently. For example, the British stereotype of having a "stiff upper lip" means that British veterans are less likely to be diagnosed with PTSD, and are in turn more likely to end up abusing alcohol and being

diagnosed with clinical depression. See Morris, "How Much Does Culture Matter to P.T.S.D.?," *New Yorker*, July 16, 2013, accessed November 23, 2016, http://www.newyorker.com/tech/elements /how-much-does-culture-matter-for-p-t-s-d:

24   *twice as likely as whites to report needing mental health care*
      My-Thuan Tran, "Vietnamese Refugees Still Affected by War," *Los Angeles Times*, September 5, 2008. Another 2008 article, published in the *Journal of the American Geriatrics Society*, found that 21 percent of all Vietnamese Americans who participated in a recent California health policy study said they suffered from depression and anxiety, as compared with 10 percent of whites. Whites, however, were far more likely to seek help and treatment: in a recent California study, 45 percent of white patients polled discussed mental health issues with their medical providers, compared with only 20 percent of Vietnamese Americans. For a good general look at Asian American and Pacific Islander mental health issues, see U.S. Office of the Surgeon General, U.S. Center for Mental Health Services, and U.S. National Institute of Mental Health, "Mental Health Care for Asian Americans and Pacific Islanders," in *Mental Health: Culture, Race and Ethnicity: A Supplement to Mental Health: A Report of the Surgeon General* (Rockville, Md.: August 2001), accessed November 23, 2016, http://www.namisa.org/uploads/5/0/7/8/5078292/mental _health_culture_race_and_ethnicity_chpt_5_mental_health _asian_2.pdf. See also Laurie Meyers, "Asian-American Mental Health," *The Monitor on Psychology* 37, no. 2 (February 2006): 44.

24   *a 2011 article*   Laurence J. Kirmayer et al., "Common Mental Health Problems in Immigrants and Refugees: General Approach in Primary Care," *Canadian Medical Association Journal* 183 (September 2011): 959–67. For a comparison with Australia, see Harry Minas, "Getting the Facts about Refugee and Migrant Mental Health in Australia," *The Conversation*, October 7, 2013.

25   *Exposure to war*   Differences between the mental health of refugees and immigrants are explored at length in J. David Kinzie, "Immigrants and Refugees: The Psychiatric Perspective," *Transcultural Psychiatry* 43 (December 2006): 577–91.

25 *One Norwegian study* Aina Basilier Vaage et al., "Long-Term Mental Health of Vietnamese Refugees in the Aftermath of Trauma," *British Journal of Psychiatry* 196, no. 2 (January 2010): 122–25. For some, especially those predisposed to anxiety, the shock of flight and relocation unleashed anxiety disorders. For others, the cultural trend for Vietnamese not to seek psychological help, especially among the older generation, worsened their mental health.

25 *the worst global refugee crisis in generations* Patrick Boehler and Sergio Pecanha, "The Global Refugee Crisis," *New York Times*, August 26, 2015. While it is tempting to draw parallels between the Indochinese refugee crisis and today's crisis, there are many fundamental differences, both in the attitudes toward cultural assimilation now prevalent in the United States and in the economic support and funding for refugees. Also, while the United States had very little infrastructure in place for the flood of Southeast Asian refugees, it was still able to manage the crisis largely from afar, with a great burden falling on nations like the Philippines, Thailand, Singapore, and Malaysia. At the same time, the United States's relatively strong economy and militarized processing allowed for the steady relocation of nearly a million refugees on American shores. In contrast, Europe, which has taken in the vast majority of Syrian refugees, has been hampered by long-term austerity measures in Greece, one of the most popular ports of entry for refugees, and elsewhere. Greece's dire economic situation severely limits the number of social workers and programs available to aid the tens of thousands arriving by sea, leading not only to more haphazard and even chaotic refugee relocation but also to additional economic and political instability.

26 *health organizations* As one Australian study found, elderly Vietnamese access public mental health services at less than half the rate of the general Australian population. A similar rate is found among Vietnamese immigrants in the United States and Canada.

26 *The recent National Vietnam Veterans Longitudinal Study* Lucy Perkins, "New Study Finds Many Veterans Live with War Trauma throughout Their Lives," National Public Radio, July 24, 2015.

26   The Evil Hours   David J. Morris, *The Evil Hours: A Biography of Post-Traumatic Stress Disorder* (New York: Eamon Dolan/Houghton Mifflin, 2015), 73.

27   *a whole new vocabulary to describe wartime experience*   Morris, *The Evil Hours*, 84, 136. Before the Vietnam War, Morris argues, we thought of trauma as only affecting individuals, calling it everything from being "disheartened" to "played out" to "shell shocked." But while we may resist the idea that PTSD affected large numbers of soldiers throughout history, the evidence suggests otherwise. Recent psychological studies have revealed that World War II veterans, whom some imagine as largely untraumatized, had the highest PTSD rates ever recorded. One particular study that focused on POWs from the Pacific theater discovered that even forty years after the war, more than 85 percent of these veterans suffered from chronic PTSD (Morris, *The Evil Hours*, 84, 135, 136).

30   *alone everywhere he went*   In the 1970s and 1980s, Vietnamese refugees to the Salt Lake Valley would have arrived via sponsorship through U.S. Catholic Community Services or LDS families. While primarily Buddhist, many Vietnamese families showed their gratitude to their LDS sponsors by encouraging their children's religious conversion to Mormonism. Parents and children alike would then also have been expected to conform to new religious customs, whether inside sponsors' homes or at the new ward houses and schools and community centers where they were enrolled. Even as an American who has lived for the past thirteen years in Utah, I still struggle to understand Mormonism's complex theology, which intertwines aspects of New World anthropology with a deeply reworked Christian cosmology in which a man might, through a combination of faith and good works, himself evolve into a god. While certain Mormon cultural values might be familiar to new Asian converts—notably, the religion's patriarchal and authoritarian family structure, with a strong emphasis placed on obedience—a long history of anti-Mormon violence that drove Mormons out of Missouri and killed Joseph Smith in Illinois means that, no matter

how welcoming the culture may be, it also places a premium on secrecy, self-protection, and a kind of end-days survivalism. This, along with the church's historical privileging of male authority and testimony, can strike many outsiders as insular, hierarchical, paranoid, and oppressive. Finally, for a young male Vietnamese joining the faith in Utah, being a man in the Mormon church would not be enough to guarantee cultural equality: he should also be, ideally, white.

32 *"I was born in a country that no longer exists,"* Bhanu Kapil, "Schizophrene," in *The HarperCollins Book of English Poetry*, ed. Sudeep Sen (New Delhi, India: HarperCollins India, 2012), 102. This line has been excised from the version of the poem that appears in her collection *Schizophrene* (Callicoon, N.Y.: Nightboat Books, 2011).

34 *"The One-Legged Stool,"* Yusef Komunyakaa, *Dien Cai Dau* (Middleton, Ct.: Wesleyan University Press, 1988), 40–42.

34 *liberate Dachau* Technically, Dachau was liberated by the Japanese American 522nd Field Artillery Battalion, a division of the segregated Nisei 442nd. Donna Rosenthal, "Liberation Day Shock," *Washington Post*, April 23, 1995.

36 *the cultural differences must have proved too dramatic for some* Carol Edison, "Southeast Asian History," Utah History Encyclopedia, accessed November 16, 2016, http://www.uen.org/utah_history _encyclopedia/s/SOUTHEAST_ASIANS_IN_UTAH.html.

36 *"Racial melancholia"* David L. Eng, "Melancholia in the Late Twentieth Century," *Signs* 24, no. 4 (Summer 2000): 1275–81; Anne Anlin Cheng, *The Melancholy of Race: Psychoanalysis, Assimilation, and Hidden Grief* (Oxford: Oxford University Press, 2001), 9–10. Interestingly, Cheng argues that white American identity is also essentially melancholic, built as it is on an "elaborate identificatory system" meant to justify contradictory beliefs: an ideology of equality, human rights, and freedom, existing alongside a racist belief in the subhuman status of nonwhite peoples. Whether racist or tolerant, the white American identity thus "operates melancholically" as

it both denies and validates white guilt, consuming and capitalizing upon nonwhite bodies while simultaneously memorializing them.

42   *assignment of low-income housing*   Hien Duc Do, *The Vietnamese Americans* (Westport, Ct.: Greenwood Press, 1999), 54–55.

42   *Southeast Asian men have been erased*   For a more comprehensive examination of portrayals of Asian American masculinity, see David L. Eng, *Introduction to Racial Castration: Managing Masculinity in Asian America* (Durham, N.C.: Duke University Press, 2001), 1–35. Images of nineteenth-century Asian American men are also discussed at length in Yuko Matsukawa, "Representing the Oriental in 19th Century Trade Cards," in *Re-Collecting Early Asian America: Essays in Cultural History*, ed. Josephine Lee, Imogene L. Lim, and Yuko Matsukawa (Philadelphia, Pa.: Temple University Press, 2002), 201–17, and Robert G. Lee, *Orientals: Asian Americans in Popular Culture* (Philadelphia, Pa.: Temple University Press, 1999), 83–97.

43   *a young Vietnamese American man's place in his new country*   Though I've found no specific information that tracks the mental health rates of Vietnamese men versus women, or Southeast Asian men in particular, some articles that might shed some light on gender difference and mental health include the following: Peter V. Nguyen, "Perception of Vietnamese Fathers' Acculturation Levels, Parenting Styles, and Mental Health Outcomes in Vietnamese American Adolescent Immigrants," *Social Work* 43, no. 4 (October 2008): 337–46, and Uma A. Segal, "A Pilot Exploration of Family Violence among Nonclinical Vietnamese," *The Journal of Interpersonal Violence* 15, no. 5 (May 2000): 523–33.

45   *America congratulated itself*   For more on this topic, as well as on the "compassion fatigue" that Americans experienced, see James W. Tollefson, "Indochinese Refugees," 273–75.

47   *flashbacks,* PTSD, *depression*   Lucy Perkins, "New Study Finds Many Veterans Live with War Trauma throughout Their Lives," National Public Radio, July 24, 2015.

47   *"keep expanding and expanding,"*   Daniel Zwerdling, "Vietnam War Study Raises Concerns about Veterans' Mental Health," National Public Radio, July 24, 2015. The truly unsettling news, however, is that if the Vietnam veteran study is at all a predictor for current troops' mental health, we should find similar problems in veterans of the Iraq and Afghanistan wars in another thirty to forty years.

47   *a strong association between parents' traumatic symptoms and those of their children*   Intergenerational trauma has long been studied in Holocaust survivors and their descendants, but the number and range of wars and genocides during the twentieth century has recently expanded transgenerational trauma scholarship. Residual stress, anxiety, depression, horror, and trauma-based coping strategies such as silence, food hoarding, even drug or alcohol abuse, accompanied by a pervasive sense of guilt or shame, appear to mark the descendants of traumatic survivors, even down to the third generation. These inherited traumas can be found across cultures and nationalities, and are also shared by the descendants of war veterans. Children of war veterans can suffer from PTSD symptoms including insomnia, increased anxiety, problems with attention span or concentration, feelings of helplessness, and learning disabilities. One study of children of American veterans of Vietnam found that these children suffered from depression and "anxiety with schizoid personality traits . . . were aggressive and hyperactive, and had more psychosomatic symptoms than other children": A. Daud et al., "Children in Families of Torture Victims: Transgenerational Transmission of Parents' Traumatic Experiences to Their Children," *International Journal of Social Welfare* 14 (2005): 23–32. For more on transgenerational inheritance of trauma, see Brent Bezo et al., "Living in 'Survival Mode': Intergenerational Transmission of Trauma from the Holodomor Genocide of 1932–1933 in Ukraine," *Social Science and Medicine* 134 (2015): 87–94; and P. Fossion et al., "Family Approach with Grandchildren of Holocaust Survivors," *American Journal of Psychotherapy* 134 (2003): 519–27.

48   *found across cultures*   Perhaps, out of respect for history, we may want to isolate or distinguish a parent's traumatization from her child's. But if there is a distinction to be made between primary and secondary traumatization, it is by articulating the severity of the initial event, then examining the ways in which the parent can or cannot integrate the traumatic event into her present life, possibly hampering her child's psychological development in turn.

48   *2014* Nature Neuroscience *article*   Katharina Gapp et al., "Implication of Sperm RNAs in Transgenerational Inheritance of the Effects of Early Trauma in Mice," *Nature Neuroscience* 17 (May 2014): 667–71. Genes essentially switch off and on depending on our environment and the body's responses to it. As David Dobbs writes in "The Social Life of Genes," our genes "switch on" to fight infection, or to heal wounds, or to send us into puberty. While we may believe that genes hardwire us for the people we become, in fact it is gene expression that plays the largest determining role, and this itself varies according to the ways, and the places, in which we live. We may have evolved this way to capitalize on the evolutionary advantage of being able to quickly adapt to changeable environments. See David Dobbs, "The Social Life of Genes," *Pacific Standard Magazine*, September 3, 2013.

48   *heritable traits*   Shulevitz, "The Science of Suffering." The kind of PTSD a person can inherit seems also to be related to the sex of the parent who passed on the genetic risk. Maternally inherited PTSD increases the chance that a child will inherit the hormonal profile that makes it harder for her to calm down after stressful events. Paternal PTSD, however, seems to be linked to a child's later feeling of being disassociated from his own memories, a potentially worse form of PTSD to inherit, as it may lead to more violent acting out. Such sex-based differences in PTSD inheritance are difficult to trace but not impossible. A mother's PTSD can affect a developing fetus in so many different ways in the womb's wash of hormones that it's hard to specify her precise genetic contribution, but a father's PTSD, because it marks its epigenetic changes on sperm, may be more clearly traced.

49   *"continuous retelling"*   Cathy Caruth, *Unclaimed Experience: Trauma, Narrative, and History* (Baltimore: Johns Hopkins University Press, 1995).

49   *what the critic Marianne Hirsch labels "postmemory"*   quoted in Yen Le Espiritu, "Circuits and Networks," in *Sociology Confronts the Holocaust: Memories and Identities in Jewish Diaspora*, ed. Judith M. Gerson and Diane L. Wolfe (Durham, N.C.: Duke University Press, 2007), 270. See Hirsh, *The Generation of Postmemory: Writing and Visual Culture after the Holocaust* (New York: Columbia University Press, 2012), esp. 4–5.

52   *Beta-blockers*   A list of treatment suggestions may be found at the website of the U.S. Department of Veterans Affairs, National Center for PTSD, accessed November 23, 2016, http://www.ptsd.va.gov /public/treatment/therapy-med/treatment-ptsd.asp.

53   *lack a high school diploma*   Shulevitz, "The Science of Suffering."

53   *highest rate of incarceration among Asians*   Erin Texeria, "The Vietnamese American Community," AsianNation.org, accessed November 16, 2016, http://www.asian-nation.org/vietnamese -community.shtml.

54   *"We Refugees,"*   Arendt, "We Refugees," in *Altogether Elsewhere: Writers on Exile*, ed. Mark Robinson (London: Faber & Faber, 1994), 114. Arendt describes the "survivor's paradox" as follows: "If we are saved we feel humiliated, and if we are helped we feel degraded. We fight like madmen for private existences with individual destinies. . . . The less we are free to decide who we are or to live as we like, the more we try to put up a front, to hide the facts, and to play roles" ("We Refugees," 114).

54   *researcher Steve Cole*   Cole is quoted as interviewed by David Dobbs; see Dobbs, "The Social Life of Genes," *Pacific Standard Magazine*, September 13, 2013, accessed November 29, 2016, https://psmag .com/the-social-life-of-genes-66f93f207143#.66t7iy6e0.

56   *four young Vietnamese men*   Details from the Nguyens' crime come from the following articles: Jorge Casuso, "Hostage-Takers Were Fed Up with America," *Chicago Tribune*, April 6, 1991; Jane Gross, "6 Are Killed as 8-Hour Siege by Gang Ends in California," *New York Times*, April 6, 1991; Richard C. Paddock and Lily Dizzon, "Three Vietnamese Brothers in Shoot-Out Led Troubled Lives," *Los Angeles Times*, April 15, 1991.

56   *"just wanted to go back [to Vietnam]."*   Jorge Casuso, *Chicago Tribune*, April 6, 1991.

58   *a swelling crime-ridden Asian population around Sacramento*   Jane Gross, *New York Times*, April 6, 1991.

58   *too much freedom*   "3 in Hostage-Taking Called 'Nice Guys,'" *Washington Post*, April 8, 1991.

59   *symbol of Vietnam that the Nguyens created*   "For general western spectatorship, Vietnam does not exist outside the war," Trinh T. Minh Ha writes in *When the Moon Waxes Red* (New York: Routledge, 1991), 100, and in that sense Vietnam has become what Ha would call a "spectacle for the West."

60   *website devoted to helping* PTSD *sufferers*   www.ptsdtraumatreatment .org: "The Trauma Narrative."

60   *"There was no narrative,"*   It may be a hidden blessing that Diana and Mai-Linh are both writers: they've learned to organize time through creative will and effort. If their memories turn out not to be entirely factual, they may at least depend upon metaphoric resonance to organize their emotions, to see one event as connected to, if not responsible for, another. They are, unlike other members of their families, able to process their families' wounds in ways that let them survive. Or perhaps this same sensitivity has made them more susceptible to the stories their parents told them. Did they imagine their parents' pasts too vividly? Did their attraction to and facility with metaphor, in the end, also make them more vulnerable to inheriting their parents' trauma?

61   *Charles Reznikoff's* Holocaust   Charles Reznikoff, *Holocaust*
(Boston: Black Sparrow Press, 2007).

61   *The poems*   And yet some part of Reznikoff's formal experiment
was to induce the same traumatic sense of dislocation in his readers.
At this he's stuck: is his form meant both to repel the reader and to
induce the same sense of helplessness in him?

61   *Hindus wrote*   Robert Franciosi recounts the interview between
Hindus and Reznikoff in "Detailing the Facts: Charles Reznikoff's
Response to the Holocaust," *Contemporary Literature* 29, no. 2
(Summer 1988): 241.

62   *risks diminishing the experience of victims over time*   The ethical
problems raised by Caruth's argument that an audience can be traumatized by listening to traumatic testimony are discussed at length
in Wulf Kansteiner's "Genealogy of a Category Mistake: A Critical
Intellectual History of the Cultural Trauma Metaphor," *Rethinking
History* 8, no. 2 (June 2004): 193–221. The tension between factual
history and a survivor's traumatic narrative or testimony is also
discussed in Cathy Caruth, "Unclaimed Experience: Trauma and
the Possibility of History," *Yale French Studies* 79 (1991): 181–92.
There are many, especially among those who study and write about
the Holocaust, who would argue that the meaning of an event as
traumatic as Vietnam would be impossible to represent without
somehow taking apart and explaining the whole of Western and
Southeast Asian civilization.

64   *war-based literature and cinema*   In his essay "Hollywood and
Vietnam," Michael Anderegg writes, "some would say that a Vietnam
allegory underlies virtually every significant American film released
from the mid-sixties to the mid-seventies, from *Bonnie and Clyde*
and *Night of the Living Dead*, to *Ulzana's Raid* and *Taxi Driver*."
See *Inventing Vietnam: The War in Film and Television*, ed. Michael
Anderegg (Philadelphia: Temple University Press, 1991), 15.

68   "PTSD *is a disease of time,*"   Allan Young, *Harmony of Illusions:
Inventing Post-Traumatic Stress Disorder* (Princeton, N.J.: Princeton
University Press, 1991), 7.

68   *Writers at least as far back as Erasmus*   Erasmus (d. 1536) explicitly discusses war's negative, long-term consequences for those at home in his essay "Antipolemus; or, The Plea of Reason, Religion, and Humanity against War."

68   *As literary theorist Paul de Man argued*   My reading of de Man is indebted to Wulf Kansteiner's "Genealogy of a Category Mistake: A Critical Intellectual History of the Cultural Trauma Metaphor," *Rethinking History* 8, no. 2 (June 2004): 204.

72   *1987 episode of* Nightline   Tollefson, "Indochinese Refugees," 265.

73   *success of the American nail-salon industry*   Karen Grigsby Bates, "Nailing the American Dream, with Polish," National Public Radio, June 14, 2012. Mai-Linh Hong also has written on this article and other representations of Vietnamese American success in "New Literary Iconographies of the Vietnam War," currently in circulation, which she generously shared with me (working paper, Department of English, Bucknell University, received October 29, 2014).

73   *"The Kirk: Valor at the Vietnam War's End"*   Joseph Shapiro, "At War's End, U.S. Ship Rescued Vietnam's Navy," National Public Radio, September 1, 2010.

74   *photos of Camp Pendleton*   Anh Do, "Vietnamese Refugees Start New Lives in Camp Pendleton's 1975 'Tent City,'" *Los Angeles Times*, April 29, 2015. See also Chris Haire, "Rarely Seen Photos: When Camp Pendleton Marines Welcomed Wave of Vietnamese Refugees," *The Orange County Register*, April 30, 2015.

75   *2015 photo of Alan Kurdi*   Helen Smith, "Shocking Images of Drowned Syrian Boy Show Tragic Plight of Refugees," *The Guardian*, September 2, 2015.

75   *the refugee's portrayal as a helpless innocent*   Margaret Hartmann, "Chris Christie Vows to Protect New Jersey from Orphaned Syrian Toddlers," *New York Magazine*, Nov. 16, 2015.

75   *contradictory attitudes toward refugees*   Panikos Panayi, "Pride and Prejudice: The Victorian Roots of a Very British Ambivalence to Immigration," *The Independent*, July 1, 2010.

75 *The immigrant as an object of ambivalence* The image of the pesti-
lence-bearing foreigner in the English Victorian novel is described at
length in Katrien Bollen and Raphael Ingelbien's "An Intertext that
Counts? *Dracula, The Woman in White* and Victorian Imaginations of
the Foreign Other," *English Studies* 90 (August 2009): 403–20.

76 *This image of the refugee as infector* "Polish Opposition Warns
Refugees Could Spread Infectious Diseases," *Reuters*, October 15,
2015; "Norwegians Fear Disease from Refugees," *The Local: Norway's
News in English*, September 24, 2015.

76 *Giorgio Agamben characterized our perception of the refugee*
Agamben, *Means without End: Notes on Politics*, trans. Vincenzo
Binetti and Cesare Casarino (Minneapolis: University of Minnesota
Press, 2000), 16.

77 *"Tsarnaev Brothers' Homeland Was War-Torn Chechnya,"* Peter Finn
et al., "Tsarnaev Brothers' Homeland Was War-Torn Chechnya," *The
Washington Post*, April 13, 2013.

77 *"the original fiction of modern sovereignty"*: Giorgio Agamben, *Homo
Sacer: Sovereign Power and Bare Life*, trans. Daniel Heller-Roazen
(Stanford, Calif.: Stanford University Press, 1998), 142.

78 *also infantilizes them* The infantilization and dehumanization of
the refugee and the corresponding sense of responsibility (or lack
of responsibility) that we feel is discussed in Bruna Irene Seu's
article "The Woman with the Baby: Exploring Narratives of Female
Refugees," *The Feminist Review* 73, no. 1 (2003): 158–65.

78 *Four years after the first wave arrived* Maria Cristina Garcia,
"America Has Never Actually Welcomed the World's Huddled
Masses," *Washington Post*, November 20, 2015.

78 *In the case of the Tsarnaevs* All following quotes and details about
the Tsarnaevs' adolescence come from Janet Reitman, "Jahar's
World," *Rolling Stone*, July 17, 2013.

79   *the literary scholar Yen Le Espiritu writes*   The idea of the refugee as
      rescuing our moral actions in the Vietnam War is discussed at length
      by Yen Le Espiritu in her article "Toward a Critical Refugee Study:
      The Vietnamese Refugee Subject in U.S. Scholarship," *Journal of
      Vietnamese Studies* 1, no. 1–2 (2006): 422.

80   *Mike DeJulis insists upon Ly's sanity*   Mike DeJulis, "Closure? What
      Closure?" *Salt Lake Tribune*, July 14, 2012.

81   *deny even the possibility of Ly's citizenship or naturalization*   The law-
      yers I spoke with refused to release Ly's legal status to me, but very
      likely Ly is a naturalized citizen. By 2006, 72 percent of Vietnamese
      Americans had become naturalized U.S. citizens; this is the highest
      rate of naturalization among all Asian American groups. For more
      information, see Cao, *H. Res. 1331*.

84   *he would be civilly committed to the Utah State Hospital*   The state
      can hold a person in a mental institution for five and a half years
      on criminal charges before a person can be civilly committed. A per-
      son does not need to be completely mentally healthy to stand trial:
      he or she must only understand how the criminal justice system
      works and help a lawyer to defend him or herself. Details about the
      De-Kieu Duy case from Stephen Hunt, "Triad Shooter Committed
      to Hospital," *The Salt Lake Tribune*, August 31, 2005, and Linda
      Thomson, "Mental Tests for Shooting Suspect Ordered," *The Deseret
      News*, February 14, 2004.

84   *recent violent public attacks*   Details about the Talovic case are from
      the following articles: Sean Alfano, "Police: Off-Duty Cop Saves
      Lives at Mall," CBS News, February 13, 2007; Pat Reavy et al., "More
      Details Emerging on Gunman and Victims," *Deseret News*, February
      13, 2007; Martin Stolz, "After a Rampage, Trying to Grasp What Led
      a Son to Kill," *New York Times*, February 20, 2007; and Nate Carlisle,
      "FBI Found Talovic Had a History with Trolley Square," *Salt Lake
      Tribune*, June 25, 2009. The *New York Times* article suggests there
      may be a link between war trauma and Talovic's crimes: as a very
      young child, the Talovics hid in the hills to avoid Serbian forces, and

a four-year-old Talovic may or may not have witnessed the execution of his grandfather. This is an idea picked up by Almir Arnaut for the AP, who writes that the young Sulejman Talovic's life "was marked by war and upheaval" and quotes one relative as saying, "I'm convinced the war did this [to Sulejman Talovic]. There cannot be any other reason": Almir Arnaut, "Family in Bosnia Recalls Utah Gunman," *Washington Post*, February 15, 2007.

85 *video on YouTube* Posted by a user called "sandybeaches1234," uploaded January 18, 2008, and accessed November 23, 2016, https://www.youtube.com/watch?v=9kFkS3mmnU8.

86 *2014 New York Times article* Richard A. Freeman, "Why Can't Doctors Identify Killers?" *New York Times*, May 27, 2014.

86 *crime rates are lowest in states with the highest percentage of immigrants* "From Anecdotes to Evidence: Setting the Record Straight on Immigrants and Crime," *American Immigration Council*, July 25, 2013.

88 *journalist Bruce Shapiro* Bruce Shapiro, "One Violent Crime," in *Best American Essays*, ed. Geoffrey C. Ward (New York: Scribner, 1996), 327, 319.

88 *The most virulent fantasy* This kind of imaginary hero, Shapiro writes, typifies the "Rambo justice system . . . [which] is rooted in the dangerous myth of the individual fighting against a hostile world": *Best American Essays* 1996, 325. It is a system that privileges the individual because it rejects the collectivism of social institutions meant to protect what we imagine are our most vulnerable populations—populations that in reality include all of us. "Why didn't anyone stop him?" is the common rallying cry after any news of a violent attack, with some suggesting, as NRA officials have done, that to counteract the effect of "bad guys with guns" we just need more "good guys with guns" on the street.

91 *After Vietnam, the number of incarcerated veterans rose* Matthew Wolfe, "From PTSD to Prison: Why Veterans Become Criminals," *The Daily Beast*, July 28, 2013.

91   *If* First Blood *makes him a symbol of* PTSD   Rambo's strength as a powerful American cultural symbol remains. On January 4, 2015, Sylvester Stallone unveiled the name of his newest upcoming movie: *Rambo: Last Blood*. The film was pulled a year later, as Stallone did not think it could do better financially than his previous film.

91   *miserable when he's at peace*   David Denby, "On the Warpath," *New York Magazine*, June 6, 1988.

94   *a major decline in the incarcerated veteran population*   Jennifer Bronson et al., "Veterans in Prison and Jail, 2011–12," *Bureau of Justice Statistics*, U.S. Department of Justice, December 2015, accessed November 29, 2016, https://www.bjs.gov/content/pub/pdf /vpj1112.pdf.

94   *National Institute of Corrections website*   "Mentally Ill Persons in Corrections," National Institute of Corrections, November 16, 2016, http://nicic.gov/mentalillness. See also Michael Winerip and Michael Schwirtz, "For Mentally Ill Inmates at Rikers Island, A Cycle of Jail and Hospitals," *New York Times*, April 10, 2015.

94   *"de facto warehouses" for the mentally ill*   Stephen Dark, "Mental Lockdown," *City Weekly*, December 10, 2014. Those who want to move the prison argue that a larger campus is needed to create additional treatment facilities for a growing mentally ill population, ideally before they commit crimes. The move is based on recent changes in Colorado, which has begun providing special funding to its counties for community-based services for juveniles and adolescents with mental health issues. Investing in these services at the community level has paid off with cuts for Colorado taxpayers, since $3.2 million of funding for community resources translated to over $19 million in savings for keeping this population from being treated in prisons, jails, and community correctional centers.

94   *would have done nothing*   Shapiro, "One Violent Crime," 323.

94   *one in seventeen*   "Mental Health by the Numbers," National Alliance on Mental Illness, March 2013, http://www.nami.org /Learn-More/Mental-Health-By-the-Numbers.

94 *to cut non-Medicaid state health spending*   "State Mental Health Cuts: A National Crisis," *A Report by the National Alliance on Mental Illness*, National Alliance on Mental Illness, March 2011, 1, accessed November 23, 2016, https://www.nami.org/getattachment/About-NAMI/Publications/Reports/NAMIStateBudgetCrisis2011.pdf.

95 *Utah's own spending on mental health*   "State Mental Health Cuts: A National Crisis," Appendices I and V, accessed November 23, 2016, **145** https://www.nami.org/getattachment/About-NAMI/Publications/Reports/NAMIStateBudgetCrisis2011.pdf.

103 *a Cambodian grandmother*   Casey McNerthney, "Family: Grandmother in Shooting Spree Battled Schizophrenia," *Seattle Post-Intelligencer*, September 24, 2010.

104 *in California on Veteran's Day*   "Anthony Alvarez, Calif. Man Accused of Fatally Shooting Adult Daughter and Himself, Had PTSD, Son Says," CBS News, May 29, 2013.

104 *a simple cause and meaning*   There is some data to suggest that our suspicions may be linked to some very sad facts. A study published in the *Journal of Consulting and Clinical Psychology* draws a direct correlation between combat-related PTSD and later criminal misbehavior. In a study of 1,388 combat veterans, the researchers found that about 23 percent of those with PTSD had been arrested for some criminal offense. While combat experience never guarantees that a veteran will commit crimes, combat trauma in the form of PTSD appears to "significantly" raise the rate of criminal arrest. David Wood, "Combat Veterans with PTSD, Anger Issues More Likely to Commit Crimes: New Report," *Huffington Post*, October 10, 2012, accessed November 29, 2016, http://www.huffingtonpost.com/2012/10/09/veterans-ptsd-crime-report_n_1951338.html.

106 The Body in Pain   Elaine Scarry, *The Body in Pain* (Oxford: Oxford University Press, 1985), 4.

109 *Samuel Beckett was stabbed in the chest*   Stephen Ross, "Shining Agates of Negation," *The Oxonian Review*, March 9, 2009.

113 *an American journalist taking pictures of children who looked like Duoc*
Duoc may have been referring to *Newsday* photographer Audrey
Tiernan, whose photograph of an Amerasian orphan got reprinted
in newspapers around the world. Tiernan's photo helped spark inter-
national interest in finding Amerasians and resettling them in the
United States. See also David Lamb, "Children of the Vietnam War,"
Smithsonian, June 2009.

116 *a man named "Brine Shrimp"* Nate Carlisle, "Suspect in Salt Lake
City Store Stabbings Jailed a Week Earlier," *Salt Lake City Tribune*
(comments section), April 27, 2012.

117 *a Reddit page he found on mixed-race children* "The Chinese mom
of Eurasian murderer Thomasdinh 'Dinh' Bowman says she blames
herself for his crimes. His white father, Thom Bowman[,] said 'We
will carry this burden with us the rest of our lives,'" 2015, accessed
November 16, 2016, reddit.com.

117 *around seventy-seven thousand Amerasians* Recently, Ohio State
University conducted a national survey and estimated that sev-
enty-seven thousand Amerasians and their immediate relatives
have settled in the United States as a result of the Amerasian
Homecoming Act, which Congress passed in 1988 and implemented
in 1989. Shandon Pham, "Vietnamese Amerasians in America,"
Asian Nation, 2003, http://www.asian-nation.org/amerasians.shtml.
For more information about the DNA database to connect veterans
with their Amerasian children, see Annie Gowan, "Legacies of War,"
Washington Post, April 17, 2015.

118 *desire and reluctance to find his father* The Ohio State University
survey found that 76 percent of Amerasians wanted to meet their
fathers when they came to the United States, though only about 22
percent tried to make contact and only 3 percent actually succeeded
in meeting their biological fathers. Duoc's fear that his father might
reject him or avoid meeting him reflects a strong possibility: a significant number of American fathers have not wanted to meet their
mixed-race children, possibly because of fear, embarrassment, or a

lack of responsibility. See Shandon Pham, http://www.asian-nation
.org/amerasians.shtml.

120   *As a cautionary tale, Vietnam has been invoked*   Gary Baines,
       "Vietnam Analogies and Metaphors: The Cultural Codification of
       South Africa's Border War," *Safundi: The Journal of South African and
       American Studies* 13 (2012): 73–90.

120   *novelist and critic Viet Thanh Nguyen*   In popular portrayals of the
       Vietnam War, its image has long been constrained to American
       and Vietnamese combatants. A new generation of Asian American
       scholars has worked to remind us of the number and variety of
       combatants and civilians affected by the war in an attempt to create
       what Viet Nguyen would call ethical remembrance. See Viet Thanh
       Nguyen's "Just Remembrance: War and the Ethics of Remembrance,"
       American Literary History 25, no. 1 (Spring 2013): 144–63. See also his
       "Refugee Memories and Asian American Critique," *Positions* 20, no. 3
       (Summer 2012): 911–42.

121   *The French philosopher Paul Ricoeur*   Paul Ricoeur, *Memory, History,
       Forgetting* (Chicago: University of Chicago Press, 2004).

122   *Maya Lin . . . proposed to list the names of the soldiers in order of their
       deaths*   Karal Ann Marling and Robert Silberman, "The Statue
       Near the Wall: The Vietnam Veterans Memorial and the Art of
       Remembering," *Smithsonian Studies in American Art* 1, no. 1 (1987):
       5–29.

124   *Kiet Thanh Ly has finally been judged competent to stand trial*   "Man
       Pleads Guilty to Stabbing People at Store," *Deseret News*, September
       30, 2015; McKenzie Romero, "Man Admits Stabbing People at
       Random in Grocery Store Parking Lot," *Deseret News*, September 30,
       2015.